A Rebel's Manifesto

Choosing Truth,
Real Justice,
& Love amid
the Noise of
Today's World

Sean McDowell

Visit Tyndale online at tyndale.com.

Visit Tyndale Momentum online at tyndalemomentum.com.

Tyndale, Tyndale's quill logo, *Tyndale Momentum*, and the Tyndale Momentum logo are registered trademarks of Tyndale House Ministries. Tyndale Momentum is a nonfiction imprint of Tyndale House Publishers, Carol Stream, Illinois.

A Rebel's Manifesto: Choosing Truth, Real Justice, and Love amid the Noise of Today's World

An earlier edition was previously published in 2006 as *Ethix: Being Bold in a Whatever World* by B&H Publishing Group under ISBN 978-0-8054-4519-0. First printing by Tyndale House Publishers in 2022.

Designed by Eva M. Winters

Published in association with the literary agency of Mark Sweeney & Associates, Carol Stream, Illinois.

For information about special discounts for bulk purchases, please contact Tyndale House Publishers at csresponse@tyndale.com, or call 1-855-277-9400.

Library of Congress Cataloging-in-Publication Data

A catalog record for this book is available from the Library of Congress.

ISBN 978-1-4964-4392-2

Printed in the United States of America

28	27	26	25	24	23	22
7	6	5	4	3	2	1

A Rebel's Manifesto

To my son, Scottie.
As you head out into the "real world,"
I pray you will continue to care about
truth, justice, and loving those around you.
I could not be prouder to be your dad.

⚡

Contents

PART 1: The Challenge

   1 Standing for What Is Right *3*

   2 Becoming a Good Person *11*

   3 Loving My Neighbor *19*

   4 Thinking Christianly *27*

   5 Judging Others *35*

PART 2: Culture

   6 Smartphones and Social Media *47*

   7 Entertainment *55*

   8 Politics *65*

   9 Drugs and Addiction *75*

PART 3: Relationships

   10 Loneliness *85*

   11 Bullying *93*

   12 Suicide *101*

   13 Assisted Suicide *109*

   14 Racial Tension *117*

PART 4: Sexuality

   15 Sex *129*

   16 Homosexuality *139*

17 Transgender Ideology *147*

18 Pornography *157*

19 Abortion *165*

PART 5: Ethics

   20 The Environment *175*

   21 Poverty *183*

   22 Guns and Violence *191*

   23 Immigration *199*

   24 Artificial Intelligence *209*

PART 6: Cultural Engagement

   25 Knowing God's Will *219*

   26 A Guide for Conversations *227*

   Acknowledgments *235*

   Notes *237*

   About the Author *247*

PART 1

The Challenge

Standing for What Is Right

⚡

JANA HAD NEVER IMAGINED SHE WOULD be facing the decision that was before her today. As a former member of a high school youth group, she had learned much about making right choices in the areas of sex, love, and relationships, but this was beyond anything she had been tested with before. *How can I possibly do the right thing*, she wondered, *when my college psychology professor has assigned me to review a porn film as part of my grade?* Without this assignment, Jana's grade would suffer greatly, but she also knew that God wanted her to be sexually pure. What could she do in this situation? What would *you* do?

Jaelene faced one of the toughest decisions of her life.

Would she wear a US national soccer team jersey sporting rainbow numbers to celebrate gay pride? Or should she decline and jeopardize her position on the team? You might not think this is such a big deal. After all, it's just a jersey, right? But because of her Christian faith and her convictions about God's design for sex and marriage, it *was* a big deal for Jaelene. After the Supreme Court ruling legalizing same-sex marriage, she wrote on her Instagram page, "I believe with every fiber in my body that what was written 2,000 years ago in the Bible is undoubtedly true. . . . This world may change, but Christ and His Word NEVER will." What should she do? What would *you* do?

These are not easy situations to be in. Can you imagine the pressure Jana and Jaelene would feel to compromise their Christian convictions? After all, both had worked hard for their success. They wanted to succeed in life *and* they wanted to honor the Lord. Is there a way to do both? Should they really be expected to suffer for doing *the right thing*? Doesn't God want them to be happy?

In Plato's *Republic*, Socrates says, "We are discussing no small matter, but how we ought to live." His point is simple and powerful: the most important questions we ask are not about what we accomplish but how we live. The most important questions are not related to what career we choose or what college we attend but, rather, what or whom we live for. Life isn't about what we do as much as why we do it.

Every day you face moral choices: *Will I respect my parents?*

Should I post that on social media? How far should I go with my boyfriend or girlfriend? Will I use the preferred gender pronoun for a classmate? Should I join a protest for climate change, racial reconciliation, immigration, or some other pressing issue?

The question is not *if* you will face a challenging situation like Jana or Jaelene but *when* you will face it. How you respond to moral dilemmas reflects who you are right now and, in turn, shapes who you become. Will you follow the example of Jesus, or will you follow the pattern of the world? Our world often says to criticize and cancel others when they fail or when they offend you. Jesus calls us to rebel against this approach by lovingly standing for truth and justice. Jesus never compromised his convictions. But he was kind and gracious toward others. That's what it means to rebel today.

Will that be you?

Times Are Challenging

In 1958, a group of high school principals was asked the following question: What are the main problems among your students? The top answers were

1. Not doing homework
2. Not respecting property—e.g., throwing books
3. Leaving lights on and doors wide open
4. Throwing spitballs in class
5. Running through the halls[1]

While life was probably not quite *that* simple in the late fifties, the same question today would undoubtedly elicit a very different response from a group of high school principals. In my experience, students today fret about climate change, racism, sexism, the economy, managing a social media identity, terrorism, school shootings, and much more. Your generation faces greater moral challenges *just one click away* than any generation in history.

Christian moral standards used to be considered good. Now the moral teachings of Jesus (especially in areas of sexuality) are increasingly considered bigoted, harmful, and hateful. Depression and loneliness are rampant. Fatherlessness and divorce are off the charts. Pornography use is pervasive. People are addicted to social media. Hundreds of thousands of preborn humans are aborted every year. And our culture seems more racially divided than ever.

You may feel so overwhelmed with your responsibilities, and the myriad of moral issues that you are expected to opine about on social media, that you hardly have time to slow down and grow up. Bombarded by endless messages of promiscuity and compromise, who can honestly expect you to make right choices today?

The answer to that question is simple: *God.* God expects you to make right choices. As Jaelene pointed out, God's standards never change, even if ours do. And God not only expects you to stand up for what is right; he also will empower you with the strength to do so. How can you possibly do that *today*? Let's start by looking back at the story of

Daniel, a young man who rebelled against the expectations of his culture and refused to back down from his convictions.

Following Daniel

Because of his boldness and faithfulness, Daniel is one of my favorite characters in the Bible. Yet long before he interpreted Nebuchadnezzar's dream or survived the lions' den, Daniel faced a tough decision: Would he unfollow God in order to follow the king?

King Nebuchadnezzar had assigned Ashpenaz, his chief eunuch, to select smart, handsome, and noble young Israelites from among the exiles. They were to learn the language, literature, and traditions of the Babylonians for three years so they could serve in the king's palace. But there was one *big* problem for Daniel and his friends: they had to accept the royal food and drink, which violated the law God had ordained for them as his holy people. In other words, they had to choose between pleasing the king and honoring God.

What could they do? Daniel wanted the favor that came along with serving the king, and he certainly didn't want to offend him, but how could he partake of food and drink that the Old Testament law prohibited? Like Jana and Jaelene, he found himself in a seemingly lose-lose situation.

You can read Daniel 1 to see his creative solution, which ended up honoring God *and* the king. But there's an important verse we must not miss. Daniel 1:8 says, "But Daniel *resolved* that he would not defile himself with the king's food, or with the wine that he drank" (emphasis added). The word *resolved* is past tense. In other words, even *before* Daniel knew the outcome, he had determined that he was going to honor God. He refused to defile his body even before he knew what the outcome would be. Now *that's* conviction.

The Cost of Following Jesus

Determining that you want to honor the Lord *before* moral challenges come is important for standing strong today. It is often too late—although not impossible—to do the right thing without developing convictions beforehand. Have you done that? Have you resolved, like Daniel, to honor God regardless of the cost?

I can't make this decision for you. And neither can your parents. Only *you* can make it.

If you do, I can't promise that your life will be easier. The apostle Peter indicated that it may be God's will for believers to suffer (see 1 Peter 3:17).

In the case of Jana, things worked out well. After prayer and counsel, she proposed to her teacher that he allow her to write a persuasive paper on why she should be excused from the assignment. He reluctantly agreed.

She wrote a four-page paper on why, as a Christian, she should not watch pornography. Can you guess what happened? Not only did he accept the paper, but he had her present it to the entire class and allowed other students to opt

STANDING FOR WHAT IS RIGHT

out of the assignment as well. Nearly half the class followed her lead. One person *can* make a difference.

Jaelene was not so fortunate. After three days of prayer and reflection, she chose to withdraw from the women's national team rather than wear the jersey supporting gay pride. "If I never get another national team call-up again then that's just a part of His plan, and that's okay," she said. "Maybe this is why I was meant to play soccer, to show other believers to be obedient."[2]

Jaelene was arguably the best fullback in the game at the time of the US Women's World Cup tryout, yet because of her convictions, she wasn't given a slot on the roster. And she regularly received jeers and boos when she played in the National Women's Soccer League.

Yet although Jana and Jaelene experienced different outcomes, they both chose wisely. They both honored the Lord, like Daniel, regardless of the consequences.

Will *you*?

2

Becoming a Good Person

⚡

HAVE YOU EVER HEARD A CONVERSATION that goes like this?

"What you did was wrong."

"Maybe, but it doesn't matter. I don't really care about morality."

"Oh, I thought you did."

"No, being good isn't important to me."

"My bad."

While you have undoubtedly heard people discuss gun control, race relations, or climate change, I bet you've never heard a conversation like this. Why? The answer is simple: *even though people disagree on moral positions, everyone wants to be seen as good.* People on all sides of a moral issue want to be considered good and decent. This is true for all of us.

Don't believe me? Let me ask you a question: How do *you* respond when someone calls you hateful? Do you think, *No matter; it's not important whether I am loving or hateful toward others?* Of course not. You might choose to ignore the comment or delete it on social media, but the idea *itself* is not one you would callously dismiss. In fact, there is a good chance you would go to great lengths to clear up misunderstandings about your behavior and motives. None of us wants to be seen as a hater.

The desire to be seen as good is one reason we are so bothered by hypocrisy. Anchors on Fox News criticize liberals for flying carbon-emitting private jets to conferences on climate change. Anchors on CNN blast conservatives for being pro-life toward the unborn but callous toward illegal immigrants. Both attack the other side as hypocritical. Regardless of your position on these issues, or the merit of these charges, can you see that both sides want to claim the moral high ground? No matter how deeply people differ over a particular issue, they all agree that people should be morally good. We all want to be on "the right side of history." We all want to be *seen* as good.

Becoming a Good Person

If this is such a deep desire that we all share, then how do we do it? How do we become good people? This chapter will address this question, but first let me connect some dots: *the choices we make are an extension of who we are.* We don't make moral choices in isolation from our character. People don't become virtuous by default. And we don't make good choices by accident. If we want to make right choices, we have to develop certain virtues in our lives.

Like Daniel, Jana and Jaelene cultivated character in their lives *long before* their trials. Thus, they were able to do the right thing when difficulty arose. Before we get into the thorny issues of this book—which will take some character to navigate!—we need to talk about how to become the people God wants us to be so we can ultimately honor him with our choices and take the right stand on issues.

Consider four essential steps.

Repent of Your Sins and Believe in Jesus

The Bible makes it unmistakably clear that none of us is truly good. Not me. Not you. Not your pastor. Not the greatest saint *who has ever lived.* According to the apostle Paul, "None is righteous, no, not one" (Romans 3:10). Jesus said the heart is bent toward all kinds of wickedness (see Mark 7:20-23). Sin separates us from God, according to Scripture, and merits death (see Romans 6:23).

This may feel like a dismal picture, but it's actually liberating. Becoming the kind of person God wants us to be begins by recognizing our own failed attempts at being good so that we will repent of our sins and trust Jesus to transform us through his grace.

Growing up in Christian circles, I prided myself that I didn't commit the "big" sins often associated with the prodigal son (see Luke 15:11-32). Although I would not have expressed it this way, like the older brother in the same parable, I thought I was better than other people because of my obedience. Yet as I got older, God opened my eyes to realize that because of my self-righteousness, I needed a savior just as much as anyone else—probably more so! It was humbling to realize that though I avoided the "big" sins others committed, my heart was just as rebellious against the Lord as theirs. I am grateful for God's grace and, honestly, get teary-eyed sometimes reflecting on it. Whether you relate to the prodigal son or his older brother, you have a heavenly Father who loves you deeply and offers you the free gift of grace through faith.

Have you accepted it?

Saturate Yourself in Scripture

Don't read this next section too quickly. *Slow down* and let it sink in. Are you ready?

Consider this: if you are a typical 15-year-old, you get 2,700 hours of screen time per year and only 153 hours of spiritual teaching.[1] That means you get *seventeen* hours of screen time for every *single* hour of spiritual teaching! How do you think this affects you?

Some people argue that television and other forms of entertainment don't affect them. But if so, why would companies spend millions of dollars on ads? The reality is that we are deeply affected by the music we listen to, the videos we watch, the books we read, and the social media platforms we engage in. How do we avoid being taken in by unbiblical ideas? Paul says to "not be conformed to this world, but be transformed by the renewal of your mind" (Romans 12:2). One of the most important ways to avoid *conforming* to this world and to experience *transformation* is to study God's Word.

Saturate yourself in Scripture so you can be transformed into the person God wants you to be. And remember: the key is not just how much you get into Scripture but how much Scripture gets into *you*.

Be a Person of Prayer

Recently, a young man asked why he should bother to pray if God won't answer all his prayers. Great question. To a degree, he's right—God may not answer all our prayers. In fact, God may not even answer *most* of our prayers. So why bother?

In anguish in the garden of Gethsemane, Jesus prays that the Father take his cup of suffering away from him. Interestingly, God does not grant his request. Then why did Jesus pray in the first place? The very next line gives us an answer. Jesus continued, "Nevertheless, not as I will, but as you will" (Matthew 26:39). Jesus understood prayer as a way of conforming his will to the Father's rather than the other way around. The same should be true for us.

At times, God *does* answer our requests. But prayer is not primarily about getting things from God. It is about conforming our will to his. We pray for our enemies so we can better love them. We pray for those who persecute us so that God will change *our* hearts. Prayer is essential for becoming people who are truly capable of loving our neighbors.

Choose Friends Wisely

There are few people in life who will have a bigger impact on you than your friends. This is why Paul warns, "Do not be deceived: 'Bad company ruins good morals'" (1 Corinthians 15:33).

Good friends not only keep us from trouble; they help us live wise and courageous lives. Proverbs 27:17 says, "Iron sharpens iron, and one man sharpens another." Great friendships, rooted in biblical truth, help us become the type of people God wants us to be. This is why J. R. R. Tolkien considered Sam the essential character of his Lord of the Rings trilogy. Tolkien realized that those who accomplish great things in life have the strength of a faithful companion. Frodo could not have accomplished his great task without the enduring friendship of Sam. And the same is true for each of us.

Members of various church support groups understand the power of friendship and accountability. There are many communities of wounded people who, despite their common addictions, choose to abstain from drinking alcohol, viewing pornography, and other temptations. They care for and message one another. They have pastors and prayer, but without one another, they could not succeed. They need each other for the strength to avoid certain temptations. No matter how strong we think we are, none of us can thrive alone—period.

This is why it's so important to be a member of a local church. Many Christians—young and old—see church membership as helpful for some and optional for all. But God has designed the church to be the primary means through which believers are discipled, counseled, supported, and encouraged. Join a good church and get involved!

Conclusion

How can you be a good person today? The answer is simple. You can't. It simply can't be done in your own strength. But if you embrace the free gift of salvation through faith in Jesus Christ, saturate yourself in God's Word, prayerfully conform your will to God's, and choose friends wisely (including joining a local church), God will help you form your character to become the kind of person he made you to be.

Then you can be in a position to truly love your neighbors.

3

Loving My Neighbor

⚡

"THAT'S RIDICULOUS! How can you make such a crazy claim? You must be blind!"

A high school student said this to me during a recent public presentation. Why would he make such an abrasive comment? The answer is easy: I was doing my "Atheist Encounter" presentation at his church. Let me explain.

At churches, conferences, and schools, I often role-play an atheist to motivate Christians to see how prepared (or *not* prepared) they are to engage someone of another faith. While audiences know I am really a Christian, I put on glasses to role-play an atheist, take live questions from the audience, and then offer my best atheist responses. (You can watch me do this on YouTube, if it interests you.)

Audiences typically start confidently, asking me a range of questions about evolution, the origin of morality, and the purpose of life. But after I have offered some thoughtful atheist responses, groups often get defensive. In fact, some get *really* defensive. I have had people storm out of the session, yell answers across the room, and personally insult me. And they know I'm role-playing!

As soon as I step out of character by taking off my glasses, I always start with a simple question: "What words would you use to describe how you treated your atheist guest?" After a few moments of blank stares, people typically offer words like *disrespectful*, *aggressive*, *rude*, and even *hostile*. Some people ask thoughtful and gracious questions during the role-play, but overall, many groups are interested more in winning an argument than in genuinely engaging their atheist guest in friendly, constructive dialogue.

If many Christians are willing to treat a fellow Christian *role-playing an atheist* like this, then it seems to me we have a lot to learn about better loving our neighbors.

Convictions and Grace

Why do you think Christian groups respond this way? After doing this presentation hundreds of times, I am convinced there are two big reasons. First, many Christians don't know what they believe and why. Think about it: If you haven't thought deeply about the basis of your faith and don't have a thoughtful answer for a tough challenge, isn't it natural to get defensive when someone presses you? If we don't have solid reasons for our beliefs, it is difficult to respond graciously when people challenge us.

This is why this book is so important! If you want to have meaningful conversations with people of different faiths—or with those who hold opposing views on issues as diverse as abortion, climate change, and race—you *must* have some depth to your beliefs. To be confident and calm in conversation, you must know what you believe and why you believe it.

The second reason Christians often get defensive is that we forget how gracious God has been toward *us*. In Matthew 18:21-35, Jesus tells the story of a servant who was forgiven a massive debt by the king. Even though he had every right to throw the servant in prison, the king had mercy on him and forgave his debt. But then the servant went away and found another servant who owed him a small debt. Rather than extending grace to this servant, as the king had done for him, he had the servant thrown in prison. The king was furious when he found out what the first servant had done. And rightly so!

Here's a crucial implication of this parable: *when someone is transformed by God's mercy, they will extend that mercy to others.* Therefore, a failure to grant mercy to others reveals we don't truly grasp the depth of God's mercy to us. The servant failed to realize how much kindness the king had shown him, and so he lacked kindness in relation to another servant.

This raises a crucial question: Have *you* experienced God's grace personally?

Be Kind Toward Others

Why is graciousness so important today? The answer is easy: we live in an angry, divided culture. Because of social media, everyone has a microphone to express their anger and moral disgust at the beliefs and behaviors of others. In fact, we are even told today that it is immoral *not* to speak out on certain issues. What is a thoughtful Christian to do?

A few years ago, a popular writer posted a short clip of one of my videos on sexuality on his blog. Ignoring the context, he critiqued me as being hateful, bigoted, and lacking in love. There were dozens of brutal comments. To be honest, it stung pretty deeply.

While some of my friends thought I should write a critical letter in response, after much prayer and reflection, I decided to take a different route. I wrote him a personal email that (as graciously as I could) pointed out some of his misunderstandings and focused on the common ground we shared as fathers and Christians. If anything, I wanted to err on the side of being kind. To my surprise, although he didn't apologize directly, he posted my email on his blog with some kind words about my response. And many others noticed too.

It is *easy* to respond in anger. Regretfully, I have done it many times. But Jesus calls us to a higher standard. He calls us to use our words, both spoken and written, in a kind manner toward others. Titus 3:2 says "to speak evil of no one, to avoid quarreling, to be gentle, and to show perfect courtesy toward all people." Colossians 4:6 says, "Let your speech always be gracious, seasoned with salt, so that you may know how you ought to answer each person." Yes, yes, *yes*! Christians are to be characterized by their gracious, loving interactions with others.

Does this mean we compromise truth? Absolutely not! Paul says we are to "[speak] the truth in love" (Ephesians 4:15). On the one hand, God's truth can sometimes offend people, so we must fight the temptation to soften or compromise it. On the other hand, people can sometimes offend us, so we must guard against the temptation to speak insultingly or abrasively. With one, we're tempted to sacrifice truth for "love." With the other, we're tempted to sacrifice love for truth. Both of these are mistaken and unbiblical, and Jesus teaches us a better way.

Considering that Jesus *is* truth (see John 14:6) and that truth brings freedom (see John 8:32), we must be willing to speak truth at appropriate times and in appropriate ways. But we must do so from a heart of love and with a spirit of kindness toward others.

Here's the bottom line: loving our neighbors involves speaking truth with wisdom and kindness.

Cultural Love vs. Biblical Love

You might be thinking, *That sounds great, but in practice, it's really hard to "speak the truth in love" today. How do I practically love people I disagree with—my LGTBQ friends, for example?* I agree that it's difficult. Sometimes there's a cost for following Jesus, as we saw in the case of Jaelene.

One reason it is so challenging to love our neighbors today is that our culture operates under a different definition of love than held by Jesus. Today, love means *affirming* someone's behavior and beliefs. It means *accepting* someone for who they believe themselves to be. And it means *agreeing* with however someone feels about themselves. If not, you're hateful.

But Jesus held a different view of love. The apostle John said, "By this we know love, that he laid down his life for us, and we ought to lay down our lives for the brothers" (1 John 3:16). According to the example of Jesus, love involves a willingness to sacrifice for the good of another. It is a commitment to the well-being of another person, *even if he or she does not recognize or accept the reality of the good.* Love does not necessarily imply that others recognize we are acting in their best interest, which is why many confuse loving actions for hateful ones. After all, people jeered at Jesus on the cross, thinking they were doing what was right. Biblically, love involves being committed to the objective good of others regardless of how they feel.

Challenge Accepted?

Can you see why it's so challenging to love people today? We are called to love our neighbors who may not even realize that what they are doing is wrong. Interestingly, the prodigal son squandered his father's inheritance on wild living without any recognition he was doing wrong until finally "he came to himself" (Luke 15:17). He apparently had fun living in sin for some time. Given the power of sin, it is easy for us to be confused about what is right and what is wrong. This is why we must always look to Jesus as our example. Culture may change, but "Jesus Christ is the same yesterday and today and forever" (Hebrews 13:8).

When asked about the greatest commandment in the law, Jesus said to love God with all your heart, soul, mind, and strength and to love your neighbor as yourself (see Mark 12:28-31). Loving God and loving other people is the essence of the Christian life. But as I have said a few times already, this does not mean it will be easy. Yet isn't there value in making hard choices? Difficult things are meaningful. Nothing worth having comes easy.

It is not easy to love your neighbor today. In reality, it never has been easy to follow in the steps of Jesus. But God has called you to this task. Are you up for the challenge?

4

Thinking Christianly

MY DAD IS MY HERO. Even though he was raised by an alcoholic father, was sexually abused as a child by a man who lived on their farm, and had a sister who committed suicide, my dad has made a conscious choice to not see himself as a victim. Despite his tough background, he has lived a remarkable life of both joy *and* impact.

One of the most significant lessons he has taught me is about the power of assumptions. As a high school student, I remember him saying, "When you read an article or book, always discern the assumptions of the person who wrote it. Their assumptions will shape everything they write."

Although it took me some time to really grasp its significance, now I see how powerful this insight is.

Essentially, my dad was teaching me to understand the power of *worldview*. Simply put, a worldview is a perspective of reality, a set of assumptions that shapes how we see the world. Everyone has a worldview. It is impossible *not* to have one. But many people have not taken the time to examine the nature of their belief system, how they arrived at it, and how deeply it shapes the way they live. Most people seem to adopt their worldview from others without serious reflection (which may be one reason Jesus called people sheep!).

How about you? Have you thought much about your worldview?

Worldviews Are Maps

To be more concrete, think of a worldview like a mental map. If you have an accurate map, then you can navigate reality with clarity. If your map is faulty, it will lead you astray. Years ago, I was staying at a hotel in a small town in the Midwest. I woke up suddenly in the middle of the night and completely forgot where I was. Since the room was pitch black and I didn't have an accurate mental map of the room, it took me a few minutes of blind meandering to find the light. Once I flipped the switch, I remembered where I was and could then navigate the room correctly.

While maps help us navigate physical terrain, a worldview helps us navigate both physical *and* spiritual realities.

Worldviews answer big questions like, Is there a God? Does life continue after death? What is a human being? What brings true happiness? Is there a moral law?

There are many different ways that people might answer these questions, meaning there are many different mental maps that people may follow. Let's look at one worldview in a little more detail.

Stranger Things: The Worldview of Naturalism

Naturalism is a powerful worldview today. It is the idea that God does not exist and that everything can be explained by natural forces. Thus, according to this worldview, God, demonic forces, the soul, and other immaterial things are not real. Marxism, nihilism, and secular humanism are other examples of naturalistic worldviews.

While naturalism is influential in media and the educational system, it also appears in shows like *Stranger Things*. On the surface, *Stranger Things* may appear to embrace a supernatural worldview. After all, it includes a kind of demon possession (the Mind Flayer), demon-like beings (Demogorgons), and an alternate dimension (the Upside Down). In season 1, Mike describes the Upside Down as "a dimension that is a dark reflection, or echo, of our world. It is a place of decay and death, a plane out of phase, a place of monsters. It is right next to you, and you don't even see it." This *sounds* like a supernatural demonic realm, but is it?

Consider this question: Who do the kids turn to for advice when they need to access the Upside Down? They don't go to a spiritual adviser, consult Scripture, or attempt some kind of mystical ritual. Rather, they consult their science teacher, Mr. Clarke, who becomes a trusted adviser throughout the series. To access the Upside Down, they tap his scientific expertise because they assume it is an alternate *physical* dimension. It may contain different life-forms and plant life, but it is not an immaterial, spiritual realm.

There are certain elements of the series that remain unexplained, such as the source of Eleven's powers. But the implication seems to be that she is more like a superhero character from the X-Men than a being with genuinely supernatural powers. Like most sci-fi films, *Stranger Things* takes place in a naturalistic world.

Worldview Affects How You Live

How you answer worldview questions profoundly influences your daily choices. Consider a few examples.

Abortion

Imagine a teen girl who becomes pregnant after having sex with her boyfriend. What should she do?

Secular humanism is a naturalistic worldview that views religion as the key problem in the world. Since secular humanists do not believe the unborn is a valuable human being and believe that the mother has ultimate authority over her body (of which they view the baby as a part), abortion seems like a good option. Why should the teen girl jeopardize her future by bringing an unwanted child into the world?

The Christian worldview, on the other hand, suggests otherwise. As we will see later, both science and Scripture agree that the unborn is a human being at the moment of conception. Since all humans are made in the image of God, and thus have intrinsic value, the teen girl should choose to give birth.

This is not to say that every secular humanist supports abortion or that every Christian chooses life. This is *certainly* not true. But it illustrates how worldviews can translate into choices.

Marijuana

Imagine a second scenario. Your friend offers you marijuana. "It feels good," he says, "and it will help you relax." Should you use it?

Existentialism is a naturalistic worldview based on the idea that we define our own existence. Thus, existentialism would suggest that as long as it feels good and you are authentically choosing it for yourself, smoking marijuana is fine. Besides, marijuana is now legal in many parts of the United States.

Again, the Christian worldview suggests otherwise. While God has designed us to experience pleasure, we are foremost called to honor God with our bodies (see Romans 12:1). We are also called to love God with our minds, which involves having our mental abilities under the control of the Holy Spirit, not a foreign substance.

Assisted Suicide

Let's consider a final example, assisted suicide. According to naturalism, humans are the result of an unguided evolutionary process. Although some naturalists affirm that humans have worth and dignity and work to improve society, it is difficult to see how humans have objective value in a Godless universe. Humans are a cosmic accident. Since there is no divine purpose for humans and no afterlife, there is no reason to endure the pain of a terminal diagnosis or to force other people to care for them. People should be able to determine the end of their lives if they want to.

Yet according to Christianity, human beings are made in God's image and thus have intrinsic value. As reflections of the Creator, every single human being—regardless of skin color, biological sex, intelligence, or any other secondary characteristic—is loved by God and has inherent worth (see Genesis 1:27). Thus, Christians are called to reject racism, protect people from bullying, and care for illegal immigrants as a way of loving their neighbors. And this means, too, that assisted suicide is wrong as it presumes that a person is valuable because of their ability or their usefulness to society rather than because that person is made in the image of God.

Here's the important takeaway: *moral differences stem from deep worldview commitments.* As we explore a range of controversial ethical issues in this book, don't lose sight of the underlying worldview issues.

Can you see why my father told me to be aware of assumptions? There are many more worldviews than we have discussed here. For instance, *consumerism* says you are what you own and promises happiness to those who buy things. *Hedonism* considers the pursuit of pleasure the highest good. *Individualism* places the individual at the center of moral authority. These three may not be formal worldviews, like secular humanism, but they have the basic structure of a worldview and do "sell" a competing story about reality that Christians can be tempted to "buy."

How to Spot Hidden Worldviews

Not only are each of these worldviews in conflict with the teachings of Jesus; they also profoundly shape the life choices of those who hold them. At this point, you might be wondering the same question I asked my dad in high school: *How do I recognize worldviews?*

Here are a few pointers he taught me:

- When reading a book (or article), consider a few questions: Who is the author? Where was she educated? What is her expertise? Who is the publisher? Who is the author writing to and why? What is her belief system?

- Consider the same kinds of questions when watching television, YouTube, or videos on a social media app. Take the news channel CNN. It was founded by Ted Turner, who was awarded Humanist of the Year (1990) by the American Humanist Association. Do you think this shapes their news coverage? Of course! (All news channels have biases, by the way.)

- When having a conversation, ask probing questions and be a good listener. Try to discern the underlying assumptions that drive the other person's moral beliefs or behavior.

People don't hold moral positions in a vacuum. Rather, these positions stem from people's worldviews about the nature of reality. Learning to recognize underlying worldviews is an important skill for Christians who want to engage the people around them in meaningful conversations.

5

Judging Others

⚡

NOT LONG AGO, while I was speaking at a small youth group, a teen girl stood up and asked me, "Who are you to judge?" She clearly thought I was hateful for judging certain behavior as wrong.

As best as I can remember, I said, "I have thought about this for a long time, weighed all sides of the issue, and think my position *is* the most moral, although I am open to correction if you could show I am wrong. Why wouldn't I be qualified?" She wasn't quite sure how to respond.

My goal wasn't to embarrass her but to point out that, as human beings, we are *supposed* to make informed moral judgments. We do it all the time. In fact, she was morally judging me! By asking what right I had to make a moral judgment, she was implying that I ought not make such a judgment. But isn't *that* a judgment? Of course!

Without realizing it, people regularly say contradictory things like this. Ever heard someone make one of the following claims?

- "You should be tolerant of views different from your own." If we should be tolerant of views different from our own, and my view is different from yours, shouldn't you be tolerant of mine?

- "You should not force your morals on others." If we shouldn't force morals on others, and this is your moral viewpoint, then why are you trying to force it on me?

- "It is arrogant to think you are right." Do you think you are right that it is arrogant for someone to think they're right? If so, doesn't that make you arrogant?

Making moral judgments is a natural part of being human. It separates us from animals. But this is not an excuse to be judgmental in our attitudes or inconsistent in our judgments, as we will see in this chapter.

Here's the challenge for today. On the one hand, our culture preaches nonjudgmentalism: "To each their own." "Live and let live." "Be true to yourself." Yet, on the other hand, our culture incites strong moral judgments: "Not recycling is wrong," "You're hateful for believing children need a mom

and a dad," and "You're transphobic if you don't use someone's preferred gender pronouns."

Unfortunately, the truisms about being nonjudgmental
don't fit very well with making all sorts of judgments about
others. Like betta fish, if you put them together, only one
will come out alive.

"Don't Judge, You Bigot!"

Though many people may say moral claims are matters of
preference, no one actually believes that is true. Consider
Romans 2:14: "For when Gentiles, who do not have the law,
by nature do what the law requires, they are a law to themselves." According to Paul, God has made all human beings
with a moral conscience to recognize right and wrong. Thus,
even people who do not believe in God are still made in
his image and therefore do *know* right and wrong. Atheists
know right from wrong because God's law is written on their
hearts.

Furthermore, people don't live like relativists. Years ago,
when I was teaching high school full-time, a freethinking
club of atheists and agnostics began at the public school
across town. My students came up with the idea of challenging the leaders of this club to a public debate on the historical Jesus, intelligent design, and morality. They accepted the
challenge and agreed that I would be the moderator. Our
church was packed!

When it came time for the speeches on morality, one of

my students said, "There is a real right and wrong across cultures. Stealing is wrong, for example, and we all know it. The reality of the moral law is best explained by the existence of a moral lawgiver, namely God."

In response, one of their students said, "There is no moral law. Moral claims are like ice cream—they're matters of preference. We have our own beliefs and live accordingly. But there is no moral law by which we can judge others. Thus, there is no reason to believe in God."

During the closing speeches, rather than summing up why he thought his side won the debate, the same skeptical student chose to berate Christians for being hateful, homophobic bigots. He repeated himself for three minutes and then sat down.

Do you notice anything ironic? In one speech, he said morality is subjective, like choosing an ice cream flavor. And then moments later, in his next speech, he condemned Christians for their blatant immorality. Do you see the contradiction? If morality is a matter of preference, which he argued in his opening speech, then his moral criticism of Christian behavior is vacuous and is no different than saying, "Chocolate ice cream tastes better than vanilla." On the other hand, if there *is* a moral law by which we *should* make judgments, then there is good reason to believe God exists.

Objective morality is not at home in this student's atheistic worldview. But because he is made in God's image and lives in God's world, he can't escape making moral judgments.

Two Kinds of Moral Truth

Many choices in life are not moral. Should I go bowling tonight or watch a movie? Do I prefer chocolate peanut butter ice cream or cookies and cream? Should I wear my green shirt or my black one? These are personal choices relative to the individual. These are *subjective* choices. The phrase "Chocolate peanut butter ice cream is the best" may be true for me, since it's my favorite, but it may not be true for you. Subjective claims depend on the feelings or preferences of the individual. In fact, saying that chocolate peanut butter ice cream is the best is really a claim about *my* experience of the ice cream (the subject) rather than the ice cream itself (the object).

On the other hand, *objective* claims depend not on feelings or beliefs but on the external world. They are true or false independently of how we think or feel. For example, the statements "$1 + 2 = 3$," "George Washington was the first president of the United States," and "Water = H_2O" are all objective truths.

Where would you place the moral claim "Abortion is wrong"? Your gut reaction might be to consider it a subjective claim, like ice cream. After all, don't people disagree about the answer? But think about it for a moment: If all moral claims were like ice cream, could we ever condemn any action as wrong? No! We couldn't condemn racism, sexism, war crimes, or any other action as actually being immoral. If morality were subjective, then there would be no real difference between a father who nurtures and cares for his children and a father who molests his children. Each father made a personal choice, and that choice was "true" for him.

In the case of abortion, either the unborn is human or it is not. And either humans have the right to life or they don't. These are questions of fact, not opinion. Upon reflection, we all know there is moral truth, just as there is mathematical truth.

Disagreement Is Overrated

You probably agree with me that moral questions are not entirely matters of preference (subjective). But what about disagreement? After all, there are all sorts of moral issues people disagree over. Here is a very important point to remember: *disagreement about truth does not erase the existence of truth.* People differ over historical facts, but we still know historical truth exists. People differ over scientific theories, but there is still scientific truth. And the same is true for morality: people's disagreements over morality don't say anything about whether or not it exists.

Take the issue of abortion as an example. Some people are pro-life and others pro-choice, but there is still an objective truth about the morality of abortion. Either the unborn is a valuable human being worth protecting or it is not. If it is, then abortion is unjustly ending the life of a human being. If the unborn is *not* human, then abortion is morally justified. Even though people have strong disagreements about the morality of abortion, there is an objective truth about the nature of the unborn and the moral status of abortion.

In *The Abolition of Man*, C. S. Lewis famously argued that there is far greater moral similarity across cultures than differences. For example, every society has some version of the Golden Rule. All societies have laws protecting human life, all condemn stealing, and all honor courage. It's as if many different orchestras are performing the same musical piece but adapting the harmonics to fit their own instruments.

There are two important takeaways in this section. First, people disagree on moral issues, but as we have seen, disagreements don't erase truth. Second, people disagree on moral practice, but as Lewis pointed out, there is universal agreement on certain moral principles.

"Who Are You to Judge?"

At this point, some of you may be thinking, *Wait a minute, McDowell, didn't Jesus himself tell us to not judge?* Now, you'd be right that Jesus talks about judging others. In Matthew 7:1, Jesus says, "Judge not, that you be not judged." The verse is part of the Sermon on the Mount, in which Jesus talks to his followers about living for the Kingdom of God. But he wasn't implying that we are never to make moral judgments. Just a few verses later, Jesus calls certain people "pigs" and "dogs" and wolves "in sheep's clothing" (verses 6, 15).

What Jesus rebukes is *hypocritical* judgment, where we judge others by a standard we inconsistently apply to ourselves. At the end of his rebuke of hypocritical judgment, Jesus tells his listeners to remove the log from their own eye—"then you will see clearly to take the speck out of your brother's eye" (Matthew 7:5). He wants us to take the specks out of others' eyes (which involves making judgments to recognize the specks); he just doesn't want us to do it without examining ourselves first. While it is right to judge certain actions and beliefs as wrong, according to God's standard, we have no right to consider ourselves better than others.

Jesus knows that we often see others' sins all too well and are blind to our own. His remedy is not to be blind to the sins of others and only look at our own but to make sure that we see all things clearly so we avoid hypocrisy (removing the log) *and* are ready to help others (removing the speck).

Conclusion

To be judgmental should not mean "to disagree with someone" or "to consider someone morally wrong." People regularly make these kinds of judgments today. Being judgmental involves thinking you are better than someone because of their moral failures. This kind of judgment is out of line for Christians because it is inconsistent with the command to love one another (see 1 John 4:7) and the reality that God is the one who ultimately judges the heart (see 1 Samuel 16:7).

In part 1 of this book, we have looked at the importance

of rebelling against our noisy cancel culture and choosing truth, justice, and love so that we can be the kind of person God wants us to be. Now, we are going to start applying these truths to some of the thorniest issues of our day. Let's go!

PART 2

Culture

6

Smartphones & Social Media

⚡

I LOVE MY SMARTPHONE. Since you have grown up in a digital generation, it might be hard to appreciate how amazing it is to have one device that is simultaneously a calculator, phone, navigation system, calendar, clock, camera, and so much more. Since I grew up before the invention of smartphones, I marvel every time I pick mine up.

I remember the first time I got an email address. I remember when my brother-in-law showed me how to search on Google. I remember when Steve Jobs first held up an iPhone in 2007. I remember the first time I watched YouTube, searched Facebook for lost friends, and sent a tweet. And I remember a world without any of these.

My guess is that you probably experience the world through a different lens. After all, you were likely swiping a screen before you could even speak! Smartphones and social media have always been part of the world you grew up in.

Neither of our generational experiences is better or worse; they're just *different*. My generation may struggle to understand new digital technologies. And your generation, because you have no experience of a world without smartphones and social media, may struggle to see how deeply they affect you. Given that they've always been around, you may not have thought about them at all!

Our goal in this chapter is to think Christianly about smartphones and social media.

Your Smartphone Is Not the Problem

Did you know that roughly forty thousand people die each year in car accidents in the United States?[1] This is close to the average attendance at a Division I college football game.[2] Next time you watch a bowl game, look at the number of fans and realize that it's likely close to the amount who die annually from a car crash. That's a *lot* of people. And many of them are teens.

Does that make cars bad? Should we ban cars? Of course not! People make poor decisions behind the wheel, such as driving angry, drunk, or while messaging, and thus endanger other people. We certainly need to be wise about how we use cars, but cars are not the problem. The problem is how people *use* them. Cars are not morally good or morally bad but morally neutral.

Like cars, smartphones are *morally* neutral. They become good or bad based upon how we use them. Do we interact with others kindly on social media? Are we wise about what we look at on our phones? Do we steward our time wisely? The key question about our smartphones isn't *if* we use them but *how* do we use them?

Although smartphones are morally neutral, that doesn't mean they are unimportant or uninfluential. Like other technologies, they shape our worldviews. Consider the invention of the clock. Have you ever considered what life was like before people used clocks? For most people throughout history, the natural cycle of day and night, determined by the sun and stars, was sufficient to measure the progression of time.

But the clock changed the way we see time *and* the way we see ourselves. After the clock, people began to measure their lives by smaller increments of time—hours, minutes, and seconds. Some thinkers even argue that the clock, because of its focus on exactitude and methodical ticking, helped usher in the scientific revolution!

Smartphones Shape *You*

Like clocks, smartphones are amazing technology. They help us, *and they also shape us*. Consider five ways smartphones likely influence us:

Screens Affect How We Assess Truth

Not long ago, I had a public conversation with Matthew Vines, an influential author and speaker who believes the Bible supports same-sex unions.[3] In assessing our conversation, one young man commented that he thought Matthew Vines had more authority to speak on the issue than I did because Matthew had a YouTube video on the topic go viral. At that time, Matthew had more views and subscribers on YouTube than I did. Does that make him right?

This young man didn't consider our educational credentials. He didn't even consider the arguments themselves. Rather, he sided with the presenter because he had more views on YouTube. Hopefully you can see how *crazy* this is. The number of times something has been viewed has *nothing* to do with whether it is true or false. In fact, since provocative videos tend to draw viewers, false videos might even have an edge over true ones. Be careful not to confuse viewership with truth.

This is how screens can shape the way we think. They encourage us to focus on appearances rather than ideas. They encourage us to focus on popularity (views, subscribers) or entertainment rather than truth.

Screens Affect Us Emotionally

A number of years ago, I had my ninth-grade students journal at the beginning of each class period. Since most of them told me they rarely had tech-free space in their lives and watched videos on social media nearly every free moment, I asked them to reflect on why they kept themselves so busy and distracted.

I will never forget the response of one fourteen-year-old girl. She wrote, "I keep myself busy, so I don't have to slow down and feel the loneliness in my heart." *Wow.* Her honesty took me off guard. Have you ever felt that way? She was able to tap into something deep, namely, that technology allowed her to remain busy so she didn't have to deal with her emotional hurt. Her smartphone was not the *cause* of her emotional pain, but it was her *escape* from emotional pain. Technology can be a Band-Aid that helps us cover our pain rather than deal with it.

Screens Affect Us Spiritually

In chapter 4, we talked about the power of worldview, which is a "mental map" of reality. One of the worldviews we discussed is *individualism*, the view that life is about *you*, that the purpose of life is to be authentic to yourself and to live according to your feelings without obligation to anyone else. Being inauthentic to yourself is the equivalent of "sin," and "salvation" is found through discovering your inner self.

Can you see how this worldview is encouraged through social media? Social media is all about *you*. Do whatever it takes to get followers and "likes" so you can be popular. Be funny. Be outrageous. Be crass. Getting followers and views is all that matters. Promote *yourself*. Quite obviously, this is the opposite of the gospel, which is about glorifying God (not self) and loving others (not seeking love from others), and from those two pursuits we find the joy we're actually longing for. Again, the point is not that all social media is bad—it's not!—but that it subtly fosters ideas that conflict with what Jesus teaches.

Screens Affect Our Identities

Have you felt the temptation on social media to compromise your values for likes? Of course. We *all* have. Sexy pics. Workout pics. Crass pics. Celebrity pics. You know the drill. If a certain post gets likes, we do it more to increase our popularity. Can you see how this encourages us to find our value in what other people say about us rather than in what God says in Scripture?

The Bible says that we have value because we are made in the image of God. Regardless of our race, biological sex, athletic ability, looks, or popularity, *we have value because God made us in his image.* Our value comes not from what we do, what we say, or what others think about us but from what God says.

Screens Affect Our Relationships

In a blog on friendship, Scott Slayton said it best:

> In our social-media dominated age, we are so image conscious that we think more about the impression

that we make than we do about making genuine friends. If you are not careful, you will carefully craft an image using social media and not allow people to get too close because it would ruin the image. Then, you build your identity on the number of people who are impressed by you and who respond to the image you have created. You have an important choice to make—you can impress people or you can have genuine friends. When we develop real friendships, our friends will know we are not that impressive. They will see the rough edges and the ugliest things about us, but we will be known and we will be loved. That is the beauty of true friendship—it sees the ugly and it stays.[4]

Quick Tips for Using Technology Wisely

As I have said a few times, *technology is not bad.* I love my smartphone, and I love using social media. The key is to be reflective about how these things affect us and wise about how we use them. If you are not careful, you can become a slave to your smartphone.

Here are a few tips I have learned that can help us honor God and love other people with our smartphones:

1. *Think before posting a picture, video, or comment.* If there is a slight hesitation in your mind, check with someone else first. Since anything posted online

is potentially permanent, err on the side of being cautious.

2. *Take a break from your smartphone.* Have specific times during your day when you *don't* use your phone, such as at dinner or bedtime. Leave your phone in your room when you're having a conversation. Take a day off from your smartphone. Biblically speaking, take a Sabbath from technology.

3. *Use technology for good.* Rather than building up your own platform for the sake of popularity, build a platform that elevates God's Kingdom. There are endless ways to do this. Post Bible verses. Make creative videos supporting pro-life causes. Start a channel dedicated to reaching your generation.

4. *Be positive.* It is easy to criticize others online. In fact, sometimes it is hard not to. But you can be different. Be kind. Be gracious. Follow Paul's advice: "Let no corrupting talk come out of your mouths, but only such as is good for building up, as fits the occasion, that it may give grace to those who hear" (Ephesians 4:29).

Smartphones and social media are amazing technologies. They do affect the way we see the world. But if we are wise, we can use them to encourage other people and to build God's Kingdom. That is my prayer for you.

7

Entertainment

⚡

WHEN MY SON WAS FOURTEEN YEARS OLD, he wanted me to take him to see the movie *Bohemian Rhapsody*, which tells the story of Freddie Mercury, the lead singer of the rock band Queen. I hesitated because the film is rated PG-13 and contains a message about sexuality that concerns me. Yet after some thought and research on the film, I came up with a compromise: I would bring him and a friend if they would talk with me about the movie afterward.

We went to the movie and then came home and discussed it at the dining room table for about thirty minutes. I didn't lecture them but simply asked questions about their impressions and insights and how we can think about the movie

Christianly. It was a memorable and fun conversation. Since we have had these kinds of conversations before, my son was able to pick up on the worldview behind the film and recognize certain moral ideas being promoted to viewers. This is my goal for *you* in this chapter too.

Does Media Really Affect Us?

It is natural to think that entertainment doesn't affect us. Isn't it just for fun? You might recall a question I asked in chapter 2: If television and other forms of entertainment don't affect us, why would companies spend millions of dollars on ads? Companies have done their research, and they know something powerful: what we view shapes our *thinking* and our *acting*.

Even though we live in Southern California, not far from the beach, my oldest son rarely goes in the water. And when he does, it's often not for long. Why? He's afraid of sharks, even though he knows the chance of getting attacked is extremely low. I think his fear comes from the time I made the mistake of showing him the movie *Jaws* when he was only eight years old. The film has haunted him since. Though it may not be as obvious for us as it is to my son, all of us have been shaped more deeply than we realize by the movies and television shows we have seen.

Movies can be an especially powerful means of persuasion because we often let down our guards when watching them. Consider how differently you watch a sermon and a movie.

When you hear a sermon, you know the pastor is trying to persuade you, right? That's his job. Yet what is your mindset when watching a movie? My guess is that you view it *only* as entertainment. We tend to view movies entirely through this lens and, as a result, open ourselves to being influenced by the ideas and worldviews embedded within them. Again, this is why Paul said not to be *conformed* (passively) to this world but to be *transformed* (actively) by renewing our minds through the power of the Holy Spirit (see Romans 12:2).

Watching Movies with Wisdom

One of my favorite activities is to show my high school students one of the most famous scenes from the film *The Matrix*. The character Morpheus is trapped in an office building, so Neo and Trinity have to defeat dozens of guards in the lobby before they can free him. Because of the video game–like background music, the use of martial arts, and their stylish black sunglasses, students tend to think it's pretty cool.

And then I show my students the opening scene from another R-rated film, *Saving Private Ryan*. This scene depicts the landing of troops at Omaha Beach on D-Day in World War II. Because of its realism and attention to detail, the scene is harrowing. In the scene, director Steven Spielberg graphically portrayed the violence so viewers would be horrified at the realities of war. And by all accounts, he succeeded.

Both of these movies are rated R for violence. But can

you see the difference in how they portray it? *The Matrix* makes violence look cool and exciting. On the other hand, *Saving Private Ryan* makes violence look dreadful. In assessing movies, it is important that we consider how violence, sex, and vulgar language are portrayed. Does the movie praise violence? Does it portray sex outside of marriage as cool? Or does it show the consequences of certain behavior and discourage immorality?

The Bible contains all sorts of sex, violence, and immoral behavior. But have you ever wondered why? For instance, the book of Judges contains stories of a woman hammering a tent peg through someone's skull (4:21), an assassin stabbing a king so deeply his insides come out (3:22), and a man cutting a prostitute into twelve pieces and sending her body parts to the tribes of Israel (19:29). Why does the Bible record these brutal, graphic events?

The Bible does not include these stories in an exploitive fashion but to show that sin has consequences—not to attract us but to appall us. Judges 21:25 captures the theme of Judges: "Everyone did what was right in his own eyes." Gruesome evil reigns when people reject God. More like *Saving Private Ryan* than *The Matrix*, the Bible uses physical and graphic violence to teach a moral lesson about the horrors of sin.

Worldviews and Film

In chapter 4, we considered worldviews as mental maps of reality. But worldviews are also stories that answer three key questions: (1) How did we get here (origin)? (2) What went wrong (predicament)? (3) How do we fix it (resolution)?

Movies follow the same basic structure:

- Act 1: Who are we and how did we get here (origin)?
- Act 2: What happened to mess everything up (predicament)?
- Act 3: How do we fix it? And what are the consequences of our choices (resolution)?

Every movie has these three acts. The reason worldviews and movies are so similar is because both are stories. *Christianity* is a story about reality. *Buddhism* is a story about reality. *Atheism* is a story about reality. And every movie (you guessed it) is a story about reality.

That brings us to an important question: What stories do Christianity and some other worldviews tell?

The Christian Story

In the Christian worldview, God has made us to be in relationship with him and others (origin), but we rebelled against him through sin (predicament), yet we can be saved through believing in Jesus Christ (resolution). This is the story of the Bible, but the Bible isn't the only place the Christian worldview shows up. It shows up in movies, too.

Consider the Marvel Avengers movies *Infinity War* and *Endgame*. At the heart of these movies is the question of the value of human life. Thanos sacrifices innocent life in order to restore balance to the universe. But according to Captain America, the Avengers are not in the business of exchanging lives, until the only way to save the universe is through the *willing* sacrifice of Iron Man.

Does this remind you of the Christian story? In John 15:13, Jesus said, "Greater love has no one than this, that someone lay down his life for his friends." The greatest sacrifice is to give your own life for the sake of another. This is the heart of the gospel! Jesus willingly laid down *his own life* for our salvation. First Peter 3:18 says, "Christ also suffered once for sins, the righteous for the unrighteous, that he might bring us to God."

It is remarkable that the creators of *Infinity War* and *Endgame*, who wanted to tell the most epic story possible, relied upon the power of sacrificial love to do it, which is at the heart of the gospel.

The Naturalistic Story

Naturalism tells a different story about reality. In the naturalistic worldview, the world is a cosmic accident (origin), humans have messed things up (predicament), and we must solve our own problems (resolution). Along with the show *Stranger Things* (as we saw in chapter 4), naturalism can be seen in the 2009 movie *Sherlock Holmes*, in which scientific analysis is used to explain away every seemingly supernatural phenomenon, including an apparent resurrection. In this movie, there is no God or supernatural realm; everything has a natural explanation (even if the characters don't know it yet).

The Pantheistic Story

Pantheism also tells a story about reality. In the pantheistic worldview, humans are eternally part of the divine (origin), but we forgot our godhood (predicament) and need to be reminded so we can become one with the universe (resolution). In terms of film, the pantheistic worldview is portrayed in the Star Wars franchise as well as in movies like *Moana*, *Avatar*, and *Pocahontas*.

Thinking Christianly about Movies

Not all movies have a theme that fits nicely into the box of a particular worldview, though. Some promote derivative values like *consumerism* or *individualism*. Some highlight the power of forgiveness. Science fiction films usually wrestle with questions of human value, free will, and responsibility. Horror movies often raise questions about justice. Comedies often grapple with questions of happiness, the nature of relationships, and the meaning of life. But all movies tell a story about how people should or should not live. All movies have a "moral of the story" they want us to adopt.

This is why we must think Christianly about them. We must learn to filter the ideas in our entertainment through a Christian lens.

Here are a few questions to ask when watching movies:

1. What is good about this movie that I can praise? What should I be concerned about?

2. Do we see the consequences of sin, or are sinful actions ignored (or even praised)?

3. What is the "moral of the story"? As Christians, can we embrace it, or should we be concerned?

4. How are Christians or other religious people portrayed in the film? Is it a fair representation?

5. Is there a worldview behind the film? If so, what is it?

The apostle Paul encourages believers not to be conformed to the patterns of this world but to be transformed by the renewing of their minds (see Romans 12:2). In other words, rather than *passively* adopting the ideas of the world we live in, we must *actively* learn how to think Christianly about all of life. It is only when we see everything through a Christian lens that we can escape the snares of this world and live in the power of the truth.

A Final Thought: Jesus Told Stories

By most accounts, Jesus is the most influential person who has ever lived. Even though he only lived into his thirties and held no military or government position, his teachings turned the world upside down.

One reason for his influence is that he told powerful stories like the Prodigal Son, the Good Samaritan, and the Parable of the Sower. Jesus told stories because they are relatable, they are memorable, and they encourage us to live differently. Jesus knew that the stories we believe and tell shape our lives.

Movies can capture our hearts and shape the way we live. This is also true for TV shows, songs, and other forms of entertainment. I love watching movies, and my guess is that you do too. But let's watch them with wisdom and discernment.

8
Politics

YOU MIGHT BE WONDERING WHY THERE IS a chapter on politics in this book. Since you probably aren't old enough to run for office yet, what's the point? If politics were only about public office, I would agree. However, once we begin to think about politics and all that comes with it, this subject is much more important than we often realize.

Politics comes from the word *polis*, which refers to "the city." It addresses questions such as How do we create a more just society? How do we deal with differences? How can we work together for the common good?

These are vital questions we all need to think about because they relate to the greater call to love our neighbors.

Yet let me get one thing straight at the outset: if you expect me to tell you which political party Jesus would join, you are going to be disappointed. While I have my own political convictions, the goal of this chapter is to help *you* think Christianly about politics.

Leading with Charity

Politics are more important than many Christians realize for two reasons:

1. *We love our neighbor in thinking about politics.* Our politics should be thoughtful and aimed at loving our neighbors so they may flourish.

2. *We love our neighbor in speaking about politics.* I don't think it's controversial to point out that the world is just not very good at talking about politics. If we're not careful, the bad examples we see can easily become the bad examples we imitate. We must love our neighbors not by talking like our culture (e.g., insulting and disrespecting) but by talking like Christ.

Not long ago, I had a conversation with a Christian friend of mine about the intersection of race and politics. I told him that, personally, it would be very difficult to vote for anyone who is pro-choice and does not believe the most vulnerable among us should be protected. My friend is also a pro-life Christian, yet because he is Black, I asked him if it was a difficult choice whether to vote for Barack Obama, who was ardently pro-choice but who became the first Black president.

He said it was far more difficult than I could imagine. Why? While my friend values life *in the womb*, he also saw immense hope in having the first Black president who might help bring justice to many people *outside the womb*. While he never told me how he voted, it was instructive to see how differently we approach voting even though we share common pro-life beliefs.

Why bring this up? Given how heated politics can become, it is vital we do not let differences unnecessarily divide us as Christians or prevent us from loving our neighbors with the rebellious love of Jesus that is committed to truth and justice amid our noisy world. The greatest commandment is to love God and our neighbors (see Mark 12:28-34). Let's choose to be charitable toward others, seek to understand, and find common ground rather than aim to merely win political arguments for the sake of winning.

Didn't Jesus Say to Keep God and "Caesar" Separate?

In one of his most famous encounters, Jesus was asked whether it was lawful to pay taxes to Caesar. Knowing that the question was a trap to get him in trouble with the authorities, Jesus asked whose image was on the coin. "Caesar's," they replied, and so Jesus said, "Therefore render to Caesar the things that are Caesar's, and to God the things that are God's." Those who heard him "marveled" (see Matthew 22:15-22).

People often interpret this passage to indicate that Jesus believed church and government should be kept entirely separate. While there are some core differences between the authority of the state and the authority of the church, many people miss the subtle political implications of what Jesus says here. By pointing out that the coin bears the image of Caesar, Jesus implies that taxes should be paid to him. But this raises a deeper question: Who (or what) bears the image of God? Every human being does (see Genesis 1:26-28)! Thus, since humans bear the image of God, everything we have belongs to him. God is thus master over *everything*, including Caesar, our money, and paying taxes.

Avoiding Extremes

Where can a student begin to think Christianly about politics? A good place to start is to avoid the temptation of extremes. Let's consider two. On one extreme, there can be a strong temptation to turn politics into an idol. *If we can just win the presidency. If we can just elect our party back to majority in the courts. If we can just fill the Supreme Court with like-minded judges. Just. Just. Just.*

None of these things are bad in themselves. In fact, sometimes they can be very good. But our ultimate hope must be in the Lord. Politics cannot fix the deepest problem with our society—the human heart. Our ultimate allegiance must not be to a political party but to God (see Matthew 6:33).

Given the polarizing nature of politics today, the other extreme is withdrawing from political engagement altogether. Why is this problematic? For one, withdrawing from politics is abdicating our call to be salt and light to the world (see Matthew 5:13-16). Doing so is to abandon those who need protection. Racial minorities, women, the poor, and other historically marginalized groups know the importance of politics. In his visit to Cornell College in 1962, Martin Luther King Jr. said, "It may be true that the law cannot make a man love me, but it can keep him from lynching me, and I think that's pretty important."[1] An understatement, to say the least.

So, if one extreme is idolizing politics and the other is withdrawing from politics, how should Christians approach politics?

Loving Our Neighbors: Christian Politics 101

As we considered before, if all people are made in the image of God, as Jesus taught, then political activism should be concerned with the welfare of our fellow human beings. In his letter to the Israelites in Babylonian captivity, the prophet Jeremiah instructed them to build homes, plant gardens, marry and have kids, and "seek the welfare of the city" (Jeremiah 29:5-7).

In other words, they must pay attention to loving their new neighbors in Babylon! As Christians, politics is a way of loving others. Rather than voting for personal benefit, for instance, we should vote for what is in the best interest of society. Even though you most likely aren't in a place to actively influence the politics of your country, this general idea can begin *right now* for you. Seek the welfare of your school. Seek the best for your friends, classmates, and teachers. Find a way to improve the lives of the people in your community. Build relationships with people who see the world differently, and care for them. Bettering the world of those you live with is what the Christian approach to politics is all about.

Specifically, Scripture teaches at least four key commitments that must shape Christian political thinking. *First*, the stranger is my neighbor. Jesus told the story of the Good Samaritan to indicate that we have a duty to treat our neighbors lovingly (see Luke 10:29-37), and Jesus expanded the definition of who our neighbors are to include people who are not like us and even our enemies. *Second*, regardless of race, sex, or age, every human life must be protected, as all humans have been made in the image of God (see Genesis 1:27). *Third*, care for the poor and marginalized is crucial, as God cares for the poor (see Deuteronomy 15:7-11; Psalm 140:12; Proverbs 14:31). And *fourth*, we must seek justice. Scripture calls both individuals and the state to act justly (see Micah 6:8; Psalm 72).

Two Common Myths

In discussions about faith and politics, two myths often emerge.

Myth #1: Good Intentions Are Enough

The question is not *if* Christians should be involved in politics and work toward the betterment of society but rather what is the *best way* to do so. While Christians have often fallen short of living out biblical principles, many Christians have worked through the political system for tremendous societal good, including abolishing slavery, advancing women's rights, building hospitals and orphanages, and fighting sex trafficking.

Does this mean all efforts at doing good are equal? No! For example, many young people today are drawn to socialism. Since socialism promises to care for the poor, unlike "greedy capitalism," many young Christians are drawn to support it.

Scripture certainly commands us to care for the poor. But one problem with socialism is that it fails to take human nature seriously. It places tremendous confidence in a large government that is not anchored by a biblical view of human sinfulness. As a result, it has failed unilaterally as an economic system. Socialism promises to eliminate poverty and create prosperity. In reality, however, socialism only brings harm whenever and wherever it is tried.

Here's the key takeaway: *Christians cannot rely upon good intentions but must support programs that genuinely help people.* Don't support a program just because it is part of your preferred political party. Consider supporting it *only* if it genuinely helps people. Good intentions alone help no one. In fact, as in the case of socialism, they can hurt people.

Myth #2: You Can't Legislate Morality

Recently, I had a debate with an influential atheist who argued that secularists merely want a public voice and are not working to remove religion. When I asked him why he is not more charitable to Christians who believe marriage involves only a man and a woman, he said that Christians are mean-spirited and should be silenced. Do you see the irony? On the one hand, he claimed that secularists merely want a voice, but on the other hand, he wanted to silence religious people who differ. Here's the reality: many secularists *do* want a society void of public religion.

Secularists and Christians *both* have views of the nature of marriage.[2] The government will enforce one or the other. It can't legislate both. Have you ever heard someone say, "You can't legislate morality"? That's false! Every law legislates some morality. The question is not *if* the government will legislate morality but *what* morality it will legislate.

As Christians, our goal is not to create a "Christian society." The primary institution Jesus came to establish is the church. But we must be prepared to make good arguments for why our views, shaped by a Christian worldview, are in the best interest of society and thus are the ones that should be legislated.

Quick Suggestions

Here are four quick suggestions for thinking Christianly about politics.

First, *realize that every news source has a bias*. The next time an important story breaks, watch both CNN and Fox News to see how differently they cover the story. Both have biases that frame how they view and discuss an issue.

Second, *recognize that the modern practice of politics is driven by emotion*. Political candidates view themselves as brands who use every means at their disposal—TV, blogs, podcasts, and social media—to try and relate to the public in a personal way. Be aware of how you may be persuaded by emotion.

Third, *study both sides of an issue*. Most people make up their minds because of what their friends or family believe. Go deeper. Ask questions and listen to people from different sides. Commit to finding truth as best you can. Be open to change.

And above all, *make sure you are motivated by love* (see 1 Corinthians 13:1-3). The goal is not to win an argument. The goal is not to gain power. Our greatest goal must be to vote for and embrace policies that truly lead toward the flourishing of our neighbors. Remember: Christian political thinking should be driven by the rebellious model of Jesus that is committed to truth and justice but always done in love.

9

Drugs & Addiction

⚡

"IF GOD MADE EVERYTHING, then why is it wrong to smoke marijuana?"

If pressed, how would *you* answer this question? At the time I wrote this chapter, my short video response to this question was one of my top social media videos *ever*. Clearly it hit a nerve.

When I was in high school, the most common answer from adults was that smoking was wrong because it was illegal. But now that marijuana is legal in many states (although not for students), does that make it okay? And honestly, aren't there bigger problems for people to worry about, such as racism and climate change, than students smoking pot to feel good? What's the big deal?

These are *great* questions that we need to think about. Yet before we delve into some of these details, let's consider a deeper question: *Why are people so powerfully drawn to drugs?* Let me suggest that, at its heart, the issue is relational brokenness. According to some studies, your generation describes itself as the loneliest generation. Broken families. Distant fathers. Anxiety. Depression. My heart goes out to you and your generation who have to face difficult issues that God never intended you to deal with.

I understand why so many young people turn to drugs, hoping to find momentary relief from the painful reality of their daily lives. Yet I have also seen many young lives ruined, or permanently scarred, by drugs. I hope and trust you won't buy the lie that drugs will fill the emptiness you're feeling. Drugs may offer temporary relief, but they cannot, and will not, fill the deepest desires of your heart. Only relationships with God and other people can truly offer your life meaning.

A Christian View of Drugs and Alcohol

There are three important points for Christians to consider when thinking about drugs and alcohol.

Our Bodies Are a Gift from God

As a kid, I always looked forward to Wednesdays, which was the day the new comic books arrived at the local grocery store. As soon as the school bell rang, I would run to town and pick up a copy of the most recent *The Amazing Spider-Man* or *Batman* comic. As soon as I read it, I would put it in a protective bag so it was safe from potential damage. I still have most of these comics today, and many are quite valuable.

One day, a good friend of mine asked to borrow and read one of my comics. I reluctantly agreed, trusting he would treat it as carefully as I did. Yet when he returned the comic, he had creased the pages, pulled out the staples, and torn a few of the pages. I was *horrified* that he would treat something so valuable with such disrespect.

God has also entrusted us with something that does not belong to us—our bodies. For us to misuse our bodies is to bring harm to something that is not our own. Drinking, smoking, and taking drugs are not only illegal for students, but they are also wrong because they can so easily damage something that is God's property (see 1 Corinthians 6:19-20) and, I might add, his *masterpiece* (see Ephesians 2:10).

Our Bodies Are Holy for God

To encourage Christians at Corinth not to use their bodies for immoral things, Paul reminds them that the Holy Spirit lives inside them (see 1 Corinthians 3:16-17). Rather than "living" in the Temple, God now lives in the bodies of believers. We should be holy, then, because God lives inside us! Since the Spirit of God dwells within us, shouldn't we do everything we can to honor his presence?

Our Minds Are to Love God

As we have discussed many times in this book, our greatest commandment is to love God with our heart, soul, mind, and strength and to love other people (see Mark 12:30). Yet we haven't discussed what it means to love God with our *minds*. In part, it means we are not to be controlled by anything except the Holy Spirit. Anything that pollutes our minds, such as pornography or drugs, prevents us from being able to love God in the way we are designed to. If our mental abilities are under the control of anything besides God's Spirit, we have forfeited God's power in our lives.

Like a virus that invades a computer, drugs and alcohol can destroy the proper functioning of its host—*you*. When you give up control over your mind, you open yourself to deception and manipulation. Taking drugs steals your freedom. Rather than living in slavery to our passions, which includes drunkenness, Paul invites Christians to live by the Spirit, which brings self-control and the freedom to love others (see Galatians 5:16-23).

Types of Drugs

Marijuana

Once a hidden drug, marijuana has become one of the drugs of choice for your generation. The scientific name for the herb commonly called pot is *Cannabis sativa*. The plant from which marijuana is obtained is called hemp, which can be used to make fabric and rope and is used in some personal hygiene products, and the chemical THC can help relieve pain and nausea.

But like many things that are part of God's creation, marijuana can be abused. While there are ongoing debates about the effects of marijuana, there are some strong indicators that it has negative effects, especially for young people:

- Marijuana use has consistently been shown to harm memory.[1]

- There is a link between the use of marijuana and stroke risk, as well as negative effects on the heart and lungs.[2]

- Marijuana use affects the developing teen brain, is linked to problems in school, and can be addictive.[3]

- People who smoke marijuana daily are three times more likely to suffer from mental delusions and hallucinations than those who do not. Five times as many people suffer from psychosis if they use marijuana with stronger THC.[4]

You might be thinking this is merely correlation and not causation. Fair enough. But these same kinds of studies were sufficient for the government to act against cigarettes because of the link to lung cancer. There are enough red flags to suggest that, like cigarettes, using marijuana is unwise, especially for students.

Alcohol

The Bible has quite a bit to say about alcohol. The Bible does not condemn the *use* of alcohol but its *misuse*. In fact, in proper circumstances, alcohol is not always a bad thing. In his letter to Timothy, Paul encouraged him to take some wine for the benefit of his stomach (see 1 Timothy 5:23). Jesus turned water into wine in his first miracle (see John 2). Many scholars have noted that the wine in Jesus' day was much weaker than today's product. Yet alcohol is treated very seriously in Scripture because people could—and did—abuse it.

An innocent drink can open the door to abuse later. Alcohol also impairs judgment. King David got Uriah drunk in hopes that he would sleep with his wife, Bathsheba, to cover up that David had wrongly impregnated her while Uriah was at war. David understood a simple yet powerful truth: *alcohol breaks down our ability to make sound judgments.*

People do things when drunk they would not ordinarily do sober. This is why in cases of rape, violence, and theft among youth, there is often a link to alcohol.

Vaping

Vaping didn't even exist when I wrote the first edition of this book. That means some of the research is still developing about its long-term effects. But consider a few early findings:

- Vaping products have been found to contain toxic, cancer-causing chemicals.

- E-cigarettes contain nicotine and are highly addictive.[5]
- Vaping is not an effective way to quit smoking. Most people who use vaping to quit smoking cigarettes end up using both.[6]
- There are dozens of deaths associated with vaping.[7]

While research indicates that vaping may be less harmful than cigarettes, it is still not safe.

A Final Word

Have you noticed how beer companies advertise? Beaches. Mountains. Laughing. Beautiful people. They want you to associate alcohol with pleasure, excitement, and fun. They are not merely selling a product but a worldview. Tobacco companies cannot advertise in the same way, but they spend nearly nine billion dollars a year to hook you and your generation on their product.[8] Be wise and discerning.

How can you stand strong? Consider three steps:

1. *Choose friends wisely.* Avoid people who will encourage you to get drunk, smoke, or take drugs.

2. *Avoid potentially compromising situations.* As a high school student, I promised my parents I wouldn't drink. I also would not allow a student into my car who had taken a sip of alcohol. Let me encourage you to make a similar pledge.

3. *If you are taking drugs, get help from someone rather than relying on drugs to escape your problems.* You can find freedom from this addiction. God loves you. And there are people in your life who will help. Start by sharing with a trusted adult.

PART 3

Relationships

10

Loneliness

⚡

I WILL NEVER FORGET BEING TOLD DURING my first year of college that I wasn't invited to come along to a party with my basketball teammates. They were going to hang out at a house near the beach, and one of my teammates said, "Sorry, but you're not invited." Needless to say, *it hurt*. That night was pretty lonely. And it stung for a while.

Later on, I found out that many of them were going to drink alcohol, and given that I didn't, it made sense they might not want me there. But I found out they were going to the party only because I happened to walk by and see them hanging out in a dorm room beforehand. Otherwise, I might never have even known what they were up to.

You don't have that luxury today, do you? If people weren't invited to a party when I was growing up, they might have been unaware. But because of social media, your generation is constantly reminded of events you are *not* invited to. And it *hurts*.

A Lonely Generation

This is only one factor that contributes to loneliness in your generation. Busy families. Absent dads. Bullying. Your generation has been raised to constantly compare your appearance and accomplishments to others, to fear missing out, and to portray your life as perfectly happy on social media. These forces can be crushing.

According to a number of experts, there is a mental health crisis looming for your generation. Loneliness has been on the rise for over a decade.[1] You might be wondering, *Why is he sharing this? How does it make me feel any better?* Well, it means if you feel alone, you are actually *not* alone in that experience. Many other young people feel the same way. But they wear a mask to cover it up, as my father did when he was younger.

Wearing a "Happiness" Mask

As I said in chapter 4, my dad grew up in a broken family. His father was the town alcoholic. His sister took her own life. My dad was severely sexually abused from ages six to thirteen years old. His childhood was painful. A few years ago, as our family was talking around the dinner table, my sister asked him to share a good memory from his childhood. His response stunned me. He paused and let these words sink in: "I don't have any."

I was speechless. Not *one* good memory? None? Rarely does a day go by that I don't have at least one good memory. But my dad couldn't think of one from his entire childhood. Although I had known his story, for some reason, his response broke my heart more deeply for him than ever before.

Yet if you'd known my dad when he was younger, you might have assumed he was fine. He excelled at sports. He was popular. He was well-liked. By many measures, he was a normal kid. But in reality, he wore a happiness mask to hide his deeper wounds.

I get messages all the time from young people who are hurting deeply, but like my dad when he was younger, they wear a mask to pretend everything is okay. When the hurt gets too deep, many do bizarre things just to be noticed.

King David's Desperate Son

This is exactly what happened to one of King David's sons. King David was a remarkable warrior and a man after God's own heart, but he was a poor father who failed to faithfully discipline his kids (see 1 Samuel 13:14; 1 Kings 1:6). One of David's sons, Amnon, raped his sister Tamar. Out of revenge, one of David's other sons, Absalom, murdered Amnon.

David mourned for Amnon day after day, and Absalom fled to Geshur for three years (see 2 Samuel 13).

David finally agreed to allow Absalom back to Jerusalem, but he refused to see him for another two years. How could Absalom get the attention of his father? What could he do so his father would notice him? At his wits' end, he finally had an idea: he would set fire to the field of the king's military commander. It worked. The king agreed to see him (see 2 Samuel 14:28-33).

Have you ever felt the pressure to act out in bizarre ways *just to be seen*? If social media had existed during the time of King David, can you imagine what Absalom might have done to get his father's attention?

If used wisely, social media can be a remarkable means of connecting, learning, and networking. Yet can you see how it fosters the temptation to do bizarre things so people will notice you? Sexy pics. Celebrity pics. Funny videos. Dangerous videos. Underneath, many of these reflect a cry for attention.

As wonderful as social media can be, no amount of likes, views, or followers will fill your heart. Neither can achievement in school, success in sports, or more nefarious things like drugs or pornography. None of these can fill your deepest longings. Only one thing can. Let me explain.

The Deepest Desires of the Heart

Everyone was affected by the COVID-19 pandemic. While the economic effects have been devastating, some of the deepest pain is relational. Can you remember how hard it was to not see your friends for months? Do you remember the pain of not being able to hug your grandparents? My kids used FaceTime, Zoom, and a host of other visual platforms to "see" their friends, but they knew it wasn't the same. They missed being with their friends *physically*.

The quarantine revealed how desperately we need relationships. Online "friends" don't fill our hearts by themselves. We need flesh-and-blood relationships that involve proximity, touch, and eye contact. We suffer without them, yet we flourish with them. Why? Because God created us to be in relationship with him and with other people. Like a watch that is designed to tell time, human beings have been designed *for* relationship with God and other people.

Jesus said the greatest commandment is to love God and love other people (see Mark 12:28-34). Our most important task is to lovingly relate to God and lovingly relate to other people. That's our purpose. That's why God created us. *Life is about relationship.*

A Lesson from the Avengers Movies

Consider the Avengers movies. My family saw them all in the theater. My son and I even got tickets for the midnight premiers of *Infinity War* and *Endgame*. Have you ever thought about why people loved these movies so much? Why they were such a cultural phenomenon? Sure, we love drama. We love battles. We love good stories. Many movies have these elements. But the Avengers movies have something else: they tap deeply into our desire for relationships.

We want Tony Stark to have a family. We pull for Captain America to have his last dance with Peggy. And we want Thor to rescue and effectively rule the people of Asgard. The Avengers movies are so powerful not merely because of the action scenes and CGI but because they are great stories of human drama, sacrifice, and redemption. Like The Lord of the Rings and Harry Potter series, the Avengers films are about people on a journey together. We yearn to live dramatic lives that involve meaningful relationships with other people.

Let me get personal: *you are built for relationships*, and when they are lacking, you will choose something to fill the void. If you don't fill the void in your heart with genuine connections with God and others, then you will be ripe for a relational counterfeit—drugs, alcohol, pornography, consumerism, and a host of other lies. They all promise to make you feel good and make your life meaningful, but in the end, they'll only lead to addiction, brokenness, and loneliness.

What Can We Do?

Here are a few ways you can help yourself and others overcome loneliness:

1. *If you are hurting, share with an adult or trusted friend.* As we have seen, the reality is that many in your

generation are lonely, but they cover it up with a mask. If you are feeling lonely, you are not the only one. There are other students who can relate. And there are adults who will understand too. Don't bury your feelings inside. Share how you are feeling with a trusted adult or friend. This is the first step to feeling better.

2. *Focus on building genuine relationships with friends and adults.* Social media, video games, and other technologies can help, but ultimately, we need flesh-and-blood relationships. We need eye contact, appropriate touch, and proximity. Allow people to get to know you. And work at getting to know them, too. The best place to do this is the local church, which is the family of God.

3. *If you are not lonely, reach out to those who are.* Jesus cared for people who were hurting—the sick, the poor, and the marginalized. He ministered to them. There are people in your life for whom a kind word could make their whole day. Pay attention to people who are left out. Care for those "not invited to the party."

11

Bullying

Should I jump?

These words rang through my friend Jonathan's mind as he stood overlooking a 120-foot cliff above the American River in Sacramento. Although he was only sixteen years old, he started to wonder if he could even live anymore.

Loneliness and hurt *consumed* him.

Mocking, degrading, and laughing at his expense were part of his daily experience in middle school. How had he come to consider ending his life on *this* day?

It started that morning in gym class. A popular kid said something cruel to him, and he responded with a verbal jab. But this kid refused to back down and hit him right in the jaw.

Rather than fighting, Jonathan chose to walk away. As if he had a "kick me" sign on his back, other students jumped in to mock him relentlessly. "For the rest of the day," remembers Jonathan, "I endured shoves, jeers, and cruel whispers from kids I had never even met. Other kids with low self-esteem jumped on the opportunity to step up a notch on the social ladder by lowering someone else a rung."[1]

Like many kids who are bullied, Jonathan was simply broken that day. Fortunately, he didn't take his life. Sadly, many do. Yet even those who do not end their lives from bullying carry deep wounds and painful memories. Studies show that kids who are bullied are more likely to experience physical, emotional, academic, and mental health issues.[2]

Don't believe me? Try asking some of the adults in your life if they experienced bullying when they were younger. Be sure you are ready to listen compassionately. Many will remember the experience vividly, even though it took place years—and, in some cases, *decades*—earlier. Some may even remember the exact insults people hurled at them. Kids can be cruel.

If you have been bullied in your life, then you understand *exactly* how Jonathan felt. Studies show that roughly one in five students have been bullied.[3] If you have a class of a hundred students, that means roughly twenty have been bullied. That's a significant number. And yet as Christians, since we are called to follow Jesus in leaving the ninety-nine sheep to find the one, we should care even if it were just *one*.

Bystanders

While most people have not been bullied, nearly everyone has witnessed it. While I experienced bullying on a handful of occasions, I was more often a bystander. I grew up in a small town in the mountains of Southern California. Since our school was not very big, everyone knew which kid to pick on. While he was a friend, and I never bullied him, I also did little to defend him, sadly. One day, I remember an older football player mocking him mercilessly during lunch break. I waited until he was done and then tried to console my friend.

To this day, I wish I had stepped in and confronted the bully. Maybe I could have talked him down. Maybe I could have called for an adult. Maybe we would have ended up fighting. I don't know, but I wish I had done *something*. I regret not standing up for my friend. I have since vowed never to stand by when someone is being bullied, and I've acted upon that vow. I hope you will do the same.

Bullies

We've talked about those who are bullied and those who stand by while bullying takes place. There is a final group of people we need to discuss: bullies. In one sense, we don't really need to define *bullying*. We know it when we see it, right? Yet researchers define bullying as unwanted, repeated aggressive behavior between two people with a power imbalance. Essentially, a bully tries to make himself or herself feel better by putting another person down. There are four types of bullying:

1. *Physical* bullying includes hitting, pushing, or tripping.
2. *Verbal* bullying includes insulting, taunting, or harassing.
3. *Social* bullying includes spreading rumors about someone, leaving someone out of an event, or embarrassing someone publicly.
4. *Cyberbullying* involves harassing someone through digital technology or social media.

It might surprise you, but many bullies express regret later in life. In the research for his book *The Bullying Breakthrough*, my friend Jonathan (from earlier) talked with dozens of former bullies. They all shared one thing in common: guilt. "I enjoyed seeing others in pain to mask my own," said one bully. And then he ended by saying, "Oh man, I wish I had a time machine."[4]

What Does the Bible Say about Bullying?

As with a number of ethical issues in this book, the Bible does not use the word *bullying*, but it does directly and clearly address the actions inherent in bullying in the instructions it offers. First, Scripture calls us to love our neighbors as ourselves (see Mark 12:31). Love involves sacrificing power for the well-being of another. Love is *others*-centered. Bullying involves using power for selfish gain. Bullying is *self*-centered. Could the two be more opposed?

Second, as Christians, we are called to care about justice and to defend the oppressed. Jesus cared for the marginalized in his society—women, children, the sick, the poor, and those who were demon-possessed. James says to care about orphans and widows, two more marginalized groups (see James 1:27). Why care about "lowly" people who were frequently rejected by society? Because, as we've talked about often in this book, *every* human being is made in the image of God and deserves dignity, honor, and respect (see Genesis 1:27).

Jesus modeled this in his interactions with lepers. In first-century Palestine, lepers were considered cursed by God. They were required to live outside of cities, have no contact with anyone, and cry out, "Unclean! Unclean!" if anyone approached (see Leviticus 13:45-46). Because of their loathsome skin disease, lepers were truly societal outcasts. Yet one leper risked everything by approaching Jesus. Would Jesus possibly consider him worthy of being healed? Rather than turning away, ignoring him, or mocking him, Jesus was "filled with compassion" and did the unthinkable: he *touched* him and made him well (Mark 1:40-45).

Jesus touched the untouchable. He loved the unlovable. Even those who were excluded by society could be included in his love. If Jesus were physically present today, he would stand up to bullies, have compassion on those who are bullied, and never be a bystander.

How Should Christians Respond to Bullying?

How does God call us to respond to bullying? Consider three steps.

1. *Everyone has a responsibility to act.* If you are a bully: stop. There is no room in the Christian faith for belittling or harassing another human being.

   If you are being bullied, reach out for help. It's not your fault. Things can get better. Please tell a trusted adult.

   If you are a bystander and you see someone being bullied, say something. You are not a tattletale. Tattletales want people to get in trouble. Speaking up for someone being bullied is the opposite. If you see a Muslim student being harassed for wearing a hijab, speak up. If you see an LGBTQ student being mocked, say something. Stand up against bullying, even if it's against someone you don't readily relate to. Bullying is wrong, no matter who it is done to.

2. *Respond in a Christlike manner.* If you are being bullied, or have a friend who is being bullied, it can be tempting to seek revenge. Yet remember, God is the One who will ultimately bring justice (see Romans 12:19). As difficult as it may be, Jesus calls us to love our enemies and to pray for them (see Matthew 5:44). Kindness and gentle words can be powerful (see Proverbs 25:15).

Does this mean you can't defend yourself if you are being bullied? No! We will explore some relevant passages (such as "turning the other cheek") in later chapters. For now, let me encourage you that it is okay to defend yourself in circumstances where there is no other option. As my friend Neal Hardin said, "Sticking up for yourself may be difficult to do, but if you are able to stay calm and respond in a loving manner, then you have every right as an image-bearer of God to defend yourself and speak the truth. You are worth being defended."[5]

3. *Reach out to those who have been bullied.* If you know someone who has been bullied, befriend them. Reach out and show compassion, comfort, and care. A kind word can make a world of difference to someone who is hurting. As the apostle Paul said, "Let each of you look not only to his own interests, but also to the interests of others" (Philippians 2:4).

Bullying is a big issue today. Yet if we are attentive to the needs of others, each one of us can make a difference in the life of another human being.

12

Suicide

WHEN I WAS A SENIOR IN HIGH SCHOOL, I received a call I
will never forget. Tim, a junior at my school, called me personally to ask me a question about an incident we had both
been involved in at school that day. The incident involved a
colorful leather hat I had bought in Mexico (and believe it or
not, I wore it almost every day). Yet one day, to my chagrin,
my hat was missing. A few days later, Tim showed up to
school wearing the *exact* same hat. While I didn't really know
Tim, I knew he was a troubled kid. Because it seemed like too
much of a coincidence, I approached him and asked for my
hat back. He swore it was his hat, so I chose to believe him
and not push any further.

That night Tim called and asked me a simple question. "Why," he said, "did you treat me with such kindness?" To be honest, I was *shocked* to hear him say that. He seemed like such a "hard" kid. Why would he care what I said or thought? But what really breaks my heart as I look back on this is that I didn't have the courage to share my faith with him then. He had noticed something different about me, but I passed on the opportunity to share Jesus with him and to befriend him.

One year after I graduated from high school, his older brother, who was in my class, committed suicide. I have often looked back on this incident in my life and wondered if I could have helped prevent this tragedy.

Suicide: A Growing Problem

We have all been affected by suicide. A friend. A family member. A classmate. A neighbor. We hear stories of movie stars, athletes, and pastors. Maybe even *you* have considered it. The reality is that suicide is an epidemic today. Even as I write this chapter, I think about a good friend of mine, a former professor and speaker, who recently ended his life. *Heartbreaking.*

Consider a few stats about how prevalent suicide is today:

- Roughly one in four young adults (ages 18 to 24) report suicidal thoughts.[1]
- Suicide is the second leading cause of death for young people 10 to 24 years old.[2]

• Females in grades 9 to 12 are nearly twice as likely to report seriously considering suicide as males.[3]

Suicide is not a small issue but one we all must seriously think about.

The "Why" Question

Why would someone take their own life? There can be many contributing factors: bullying, failure, shame, financial loss, anger, revenge, loneliness, disappointment, substance abuse, broken relationships, and the list goes on. Ultimately, the issue of suicide boils down to people losing hope and falsely believing they are better off dead: "It became the only thing left I could do."

But what about mental illness? While this is an important factor, 54 percent of people who die by suicide have not been diagnosed with a mental illness.[4] Some of these people may have had a mental illness, but without evidence we can't simply assume they did. As my friend Jonathan Noyes notes, suicide rates have increased during the same time we've experienced significant improvements in psychiatric care. He explains:

> We're able to treat anxiety, depression, schizophrenia, multiple personality disorder, and just about everything else more effectively than at any other time in human history. Today, right now, we have a better understanding of how the brain works

than we ever had, yet that rate of suicide continues to skyrocket. With these advances in science and medicine and technology, shouldn't we expect to see the suicide rates declining?[5]

Yes, we should. But we don't. While mental illness is an important factor, I believe that suicide is primarily a spiritual problem. People who are suicidal are asking—whether they fully realize it or not—deep questions such as, *Does my life have any meaning? Can I be forgiven? Am I loved? Is there any hope beyond my current pain?*

As Jonathan notes, we have seen suicide rates rise at the same time Judeo-Christian influences have declined in our culture. Is this merely a coincidence? I doubt it. As you will recall, *naturalism* and its offshoot worldviews are prevalent in today's culture and media. Naturalism is the idea that God does not exist and that everything can be explained by physical forces. Thus, God is a delusion, humans have no real value, death is the end, and life has no purpose. Some people get hurt and others get lucky. Atheist Richard Dawkins concludes, "The universe we observe has precisely the properties we should expect if there is, at bottom, no design, no purpose, no evil and no good, nothing but blind, pitiless indifference."[6]

Simply put, naturalism teaches that you are a cosmic accident. What a depressing view of life!

Those who subscribe to a naturalistic worldview might then be tempted to think, *Well, if God is not real, then I might as well live for pleasure. Why not get famous before I die? After all, I only live once.* The apostle Paul anticipates this response, which is why he says that if there is no resurrection from the dead, "Let us eat and drink, for tomorrow we die" (1 Corinthians 15:32). Living for the moment can be fun and pleasurable for a season, but what happens when the excitement runs out? Just ask Solomon. He experienced every pleasure the world has to offer—sex, wine, riches, power, fame, and so on—yet he "hated life" (Ecclesiastes 2:17). Living for today turns out to be a dead end.

Compared to naturalism, Christianity offers real hope. Jesus offers forgiveness, purpose, and genuine community. Jesus offers meaning in this life and hope for the next. Even if you don't feel like it, you are made in the image of God and have infinite worth. The worldview clash between naturalism and Christianity could not be starker.

Can a Christian Who Commits Suicide Go to Heaven?

People ask me all the time about whether Christians who commit suicide can go to heaven. We'll consider this question in a moment, but first, please keep something in mind: while God has unmistakable grace for people struggling with suicidal thoughts, we must realize that taking your life is a big deal. As I have said many times in this book, everyone is made in the image of God and has infinite worth. While we can understand that people who are hurting might entertain the idea of ending their lives, we must do everything we can to stop them from doing so. Suicide is sometimes downplayed today, but for Christians, it is an absolute tragedy. The person struggling with suicidal ideas is both hurting *and* the victim of the idea that taking their life will end their pain. As Christians, we know there is always hope in Jesus Christ.

Still, the question of whether a Christian who commits suicide can still go to heaven is worth considering. Here's how a conversation on this subject might go:

Questioner: Can a Christian who commits suicide go to heaven?

Me: Based on what we see in Scripture, I think so.

Questioner: Isn't suicide an unforgivable sin?

Me: There's no biblical warrant for thinking the "blasphemy of the Holy Spirit" is suicide.[7]

Questioner: But suicide is murder.

Me: True, but God forgave King David for murder, right? (See 2 Samuel 12:9, 13.) Then he can forgive someone who unjustly takes their own life.

Questioner: But David repented. Those who commit suicide can't repent.

Me: Yes, but when people believe in Jesus, he pays for all of their sins—past, present, and future. If a Christian lies to her parents and then dies in a car crash driving to school, she is still forgiven, right?

Questioner: But how can a genuine Christian lose hope?

Me: We live in a world that has been deeply rocked by sin. The apostle Paul warns Christians not to be "conformed to this world" (Romans 12:2) because even Christians are susceptible to the manipulation of Satan, the father of lies.

Conversations are not always this straightforward, of course. And the debate could go on. But here's the bottom line: the recipe for eternal life is experiencing God's grace by faith in Jesus Christ (see Ephesians 2:8-9). Salvation comes not through our works but because of what Christ has done for us. I believe claiming that Christians who commit suicide cannot be saved threatens to place salvation in our efforts rather than God's grace.

What Can We Do?

As I said, suicide is an epidemic in our country. Here are some things you can do to help:

1. *If you are having suicidal thoughts, know that you are not alone.* When we are hurting, it is natural to feel like we are all alone. It is tempting to feel like no one understands. But this is not true. As we saw above, many young people today struggle with suicidal thoughts. Even Moses (see Numbers 11:14-15), Elijah (see 1 Kings 19:4), and Jonah (see Jonah 4:8) were brought to such dark places that they desired to end their lives. Please don't buy the lie that you are alone.

2. *If you are having suicidal thoughts, talk with someone.* The most important step is to share your hurt with a parent, teacher, coach, or other trusted adult. Or call the suicide prevention hotline: (800) 273-8255. If it is hard for you to do it alone, enlist a friend to help. But *please* don't bury your hurt inside. It won't magically go away. If you get help, I promise you things can get better.

3. *Look to help others who are hurting.* People often give signs that they are having suicidal thoughts. Aggressive behavior. Preoccupation with death. Substance abuse. Depression. Mood changes. If you see or hear someone talking about ending their life, take it seriously. Err on the side of telling a leader. It is no exaggeration to say that you could make the difference between life and death.

13

Assisted Suicide

⚡

"WHEN ANIMALS SUFFER, we often put them out of their misery. Why not do the same for human beings?"

I remember the first time I heard this argument. It caught me off guard. After all, we *do* consider it merciful to "put down" a dog when it is old and frail. Why not extend the same mercy and compassion to our loved ones when we can't remove *their* suffering?

After reflecting on it for a while, I finally came to the answer: *human beings are not animals*. We don't treat people like we do animals (at least we *shouldn't*). We don't tie people up or put them on leashes to make sure they don't run away. They don't sleep outside in a tiny house. Animals are certainly wonderful companions, and we should care for them,

A REBEL'S MANIFESTO

but we are called to *love* our neighbors. What's the difference?
Stephanie Connors explains:

> When we put a pet down, we do so because their
> usefulness in our lives is outweighed by harms (such
> as poor health that cannot be corrected at all or
> without great expense, or because there isn't a home
> for them and they will be a nuisance to society, etc.).
> Humans, however, should not be valued from the
> perspective of usefulness.[1]

As we have seen throughout this book, the Bible teaches
that humans are *uniquely* made in the image of God and thus
have inherent, infinite dignity, value, and worth (see Genesis
1:27). Animals are valuable beings, but humans are the pin-
nacle of God's good creation, made in God's own image. And
our greatest call is to love God and love people.

Yet the problem is that sin has entered the world and
brought death (see Romans 5:12). As Christians, we know
that the resurrection of Jesus has ultimately conquered death.
But we still live in a world in which death is a reality. Unless
Jesus comes back soon, all of us are going to die. Like it or
not, death is inescapable.

Suicide vs. Assisted Suicide

If you saw someone on a bridge about to commit suicide,
what would you do? Obviously, you would try to intervene

and stop them, even though they'd want to die. As a society, we generally decry suicide. But ironically, when we put "assisted" in front of it and we help people end their lives, many people consider it an act of compassion. Yet murder is murder regardless of age or health.

I have deep compassion for people who are hurting. I can understand that some people are in such emotional or physical pain that they no longer want to live. But because God is sovereign over life and death and we have the obligation not to take innocent life, *we should never help people commit suicide*. There is a better way to deal with suffering.

This simple principle can help guide us through this difficult issue. Let's begin by defining some key terms.

Defining Our Terms

There are three important terms to understand. First, *physician-assisted suicide* (PAS) is when a doctor provides the means for a patient to end his or her life. Typically, this is done by giving the patient a lethal drug to ingest. In these cases, it is the drug that kills and not the underlying disease or condition.

Second, *euthanasia* is when the doctor is more directly involved. Euthanasia technically means "good death" and occurs when a doctor actively helps the suffering patient die. Often this involves the injection of a lethal drug by the doctor directly into the patient. Thus, the doctor kills the patient. Although the means may be different, euthanasia is morally equivalent to a doctor suffocating the patient with a pillow.

This raises a troubling question: Do we really want our caretakers *actively* supporting death? Doesn't it strike you as problematic that doctors, who are supposed to care for patients and cure them, are asked to help *kill* patients in both physician-assisted suicide and euthanasia?

Third, there is a difference between killing and letting something die. *Killing* involves actively taking someone's life, such as with PAS or euthanasia. To *let die* is to passively allow someone to die from other causes without interference. Although killing is never right, there may be times when it is permissible to let someone die, such as when there is no reasonable hope of recovery and the person has expressed his or her wishes to not receive life-prolonging treatment.[2]

My own perspective may be helpful. If I ever experienced a terminal illness in an unconscious state and had no reasonable chance of recovery, I would not want huge amounts of expense and effort paid to prolong my impending death. I would rather be *allowed* to die and go to heaven. Wouldn't you?

Let's consider three big reasons people have for supporting assisted suicide.

Reason #1: "People Should Be Able to Die with Dignity"

Have you ever spent time with someone who is fully dependent on others to be fed and changed? I have. It's understandable that people would prefer not to die in such a state—people don't like to feel as if they're being a burden to someone else. But has a person who died naturally in this manner lost his or her dignity? No way!

Claiming that people lose dignity because of how they die or how much assistance they require sends the message that people who die naturally or need a lot of help are undignified and a "burden on society." What a *tragic* message to send to such vulnerable people. Dignity is not something we gain or lose based on our "usefulness" or abilities but something we all have because of our shared humanity. We should treat terminally ill people with honor, respect, and care *because* of their dignity.

Consider a beautiful painting covered with dust. Does it lose its value because its beauty is covered? Of course not. Rather, we treat it respectfully as a recognition of its underlying value. The same ought to apply to how we treat human beings—and especially those who are sick.

Reason #2: "People Have Bodily Autonomy"

Do people have a right to die? After all, if it's your body, can't you do what you want with it? We believe people should be able to make decisions about their careers, hobbies, relationships, and so on. So why can't people do whatever they want with their bodies?

The reality is that we all recognize limits on the use

of our bodies. I don't have the freedom to swing my fists anywhere without regard for your face. And you don't have the freedom to drive on the sidewalk. We all recognize limits to the use of our bodies. We try to stop people from committing suicide because they harm themselves and will most likely deeply hurt those who love them and depend on them.

But let's imagine for a moment that we have the right to die. What would follow? If so, *everyone* would have the same right. And we couldn't limit the right to die to the elderly or sick but would have to aid *anyone* who wants to die for *any* reason whatsoever. I doubt most people would agree to this.

Reason #3: "Assisted Suicide Is Compassionate"

In his letter to the Colossians, Paul says to have "compassionate hearts" (3:12). Given the importance of compassion and the depth of suffering some people experience, isn't it compassionate to help people die more quickly rather than experience prolonged suffering?

This is a powerful *emotional* argument. Yet the reality is that nearly every patient today can have their pain managed through medication and treatment. In a few cases, when the pain is unbearable, patients may take medication to relieve pain even if it hastens death. But this is not assisted suicide because the *intent* is to relieve pain. In other words, a person might take a medication to relieve suffering that may also hasten death. But it is not assisted suicide because the purpose is relieving pain, not causing death.

The Bible instructs us to be compassionate, and it *also* commands us not to take innocent life. Compassion involves showing concern and care when others are suffering. We must find a way to care for people compassionately without taking their lives into our own hands. Real compassion is not killing someone but caring for them through their suffering.

Does Assisted Suicide Lead to a Slippery Slope?

One of the strongest arguments against assisted suicide, to my mind, recognizes the "slippery slope" that cultures who embrace it often "slide" down. Consider a pressing question: Will the right to die become a *duty* to die? As older generations retire and medical expenses increase, will there be pressure on older or sick people to "do their duty" and die? Will older family members have to "justify" their existence? These are not unrealistic concerns.

Once assisted suicide is approved, the pool of those who qualify for it tends to expand. Consider the Netherlands. Right now, one person is put to death without consent (primarily elderly persons) for every three or four who give consent.[3] Kids as young as twelve years old are potential candidates for euthanasia. One in five Dutch doctors would help physically healthy people who are "tired of living" die.[4]

There is good precedent for believing that cultures that

legalize assisted suicide slide further and further down the "slippery slope."

What Can We Do?

Consider two things that Christians can do.

First, *be careful with your words*. Rather than using words like *vegetable* or referring to people as a "drain on resources" or in terms that focus on their usefulness or ability, talk about people in a humanizing way. Choose language that reflects their inherent human dignity and value.

Second, *love people when they are hurting*. Rather than responding to suffering by supporting assisted suicide, choose to love people sacrificially. This can mean different things depending on the situation. It may mean reading Scripture to someone in the hospital. It may mean playing cards with them. It may mean watching old sitcoms or movies. It may mean running errands for someone. It may mean praying for someone. And it may mean simply being present with someone in the final moments of their life.

14

Racial Tension

⚡

WHEN I WROTE THE FIRST EDITION of this book in the early 2000s, I discussed pressing moral issues like drugs, marriage, and war. But I didn't discuss issues such as transgender identities, artificial intelligence, or race. It makes sense *not* to discuss these first two issues since they've cropped up more recently, but why not a chapter on race? After all, it has been an issue in the United States since its founding.

The honest answer is that it didn't cross my mind. It didn't *feel* like a pressing issue to me or my students. Looking back, it's embarrassing that I didn't include it. How could I not see how big of an issue race has been throughout our history *and* how it continues to be a pressing moral issue today? What was I thinking (or *not* thinking, to be more precise)?

Obviously, I can't change the past. But I won't make that mistake again.

There is an advantage in growing up in the majority race in a society. It often didn't cross my mind, for example, that people might treat me differently because of my race. But this is not the case for many of my minority friends who think regularly about how to navigate their jobs, education, and relationships through the lens of race.

Here is my hope for this chapter: if we are going to love our neighbors from different ethnic backgrounds, as Jesus taught in the Parable of the Good Samaritan, we must be willing to truthfully assess our hearts regarding race. We must *each* be vulnerable, honest, and willing to consider our blind spots. And we must commit to being part of the solution, not the problem.

Are you willing?

A Biblical View of Race and Diversity

There are three clear teachings from the Bible to consider as we think about racism.

God Valued Diversity in the Past

Scripture begins with the creation of the first couple, Adam and Eve, who became the parents of everyone (see Genesis 1–2). This means that all human beings, regardless of ethnicity, national boundary, or skin color, are made in the image of God and reflect their Creator. When God made a covenant with Abraham, the goal was that "*all* the families of the earth shall be blessed" (Genesis 12:3, emphasis added).

God Values Diversity in the Present

God continues to value diversity today. On the day of Pentecost, which marked the beginning of the church, the Holy Spirit enabled people from different countries and people groups to understand the gospel (see Acts 2:5-11). Why? Because the church is meant for young and old, male and female, and *all races of people.*

God Will Value Diversity in the Future

In Revelation 7:9, John describes a future state consisting of a great multitude of people standing before God's throne "from every nation, from all tribes and peoples and languages." Heaven will be a beautifully diverse place.

If God so values diversity in the past, present, and future, then we, too, should value diversity and abhor anything that devalues or rejects people of other races.

The Evils of Racism

When you see that God values diversity in the past, present, and future, can you understand why racism is so evil? Consider white supremacy, the idea that white-skinned people are superior to people of other races. Such prejudice has led to immeasurable harm. It breaks the two greatest commandments—to love God and to love others.

How so?

My friend Thaddeus Williams explains, "[Racism] worships and serves the created things rather than the Creator. Racism, therefore, is not merely horizontally unjust—depriving other creatures what they are due; it is also vertically unjust—failing to give the Creator his due by making race an ultimate object of devotion."[1] Rather than focusing on our common human value, racism treats other human beings unjustly by failing to recognize the dignity they deserve as image-bearers of God. Racism is thus a failure to love our neighbor *and* to love the God who made all human beings, regardless of race, with inherent dignity.

Black Lives Matter

When nationwide protests erupted over the death of George Floyd in the summer of 2020, my son and I had a lengthy talk with one of his coaches, a Black man who grew up in the inner city, to get his perspective on the events. He shared stories of being pulled over by the same cop—repeatedly—because he lived in a predominantly White neighborhood. He shared examples of painful comments directed toward him because of his race. Needless to say, it was eye-opening and heartbreaking.

The reality is that many Black people who have done no wrong live in fear in America today. Many have become accustomed to being looked at with suspicion and being treated differently because of the color of their skin.

This pain has been one of the driving forces behind the Black Lives Matter movement. While Christians can and should have deep concerns about the *organization* Black Lives Matter,[2] the statement that Black lives matter reflects a plea for people to be valued equally alongside other human beings. This plea has existed *long* before 2013, when the organization was formed. Are we listening?

Avoiding Two Cultural Myths

When it comes to thinking about race, it is important to avoid two cultural myths.

Myth #1: Racism Is Nowhere

It is a myth that racism doesn't exist. Certain individuals are racist. Don't believe me? Just follow racial discussions on social media! Enough said.

Whether it is possible to identify intentional *institutional* racism or not, there are structural issues that must also be addressed. Many minority children are trapped in failing schools. It is not uncommon to hear stories of racial stereotyping in our immigration system. And many argue that our prison system, which incarcerates a disproportionate percentage of minorities, needs radical restoration. Racial prejudice exists and can infect both individuals and systems.

Myth #2: Racism Is Everywhere

It is also a myth that racism is everywhere. Rather than following the evidence wherever it leads, some people *begin* with the assumption that disparity equals discrimination. But according to Thomas Sowell, a Black professor at Stanford University, such an analysis is too simplistic. He cites the example, from the early 2000s, of how the media proclaimed racial discrimination when it was discovered that Black applicants were being rejected more frequently for housing loans than White applicants.

Ironically, however, it turns out that White applicants were rejected more frequently than Asian American applicants. And Black-owned banks turned down Black mortgage applicants at a higher rate than White-owned banks.[3] Disparity does not always equal discrimination. Be careful reading race into a situation when it may not be the defining factor.

Avoiding Two More Traps

Racism is not just an American issue. In some fashion or another, it affects every country in the world. Yet in America, there are two traps people can fall into.

Trap #1: Ignoring America's Checkered Past

One trap is to ignore America's checkered past. It is profoundly sad—and ironic—that slavery existed in a country that proclaimed freedom for all. The Declaration of Independence proclaims that "all men are created equal," and yet slaves were brought to America as early as the seventeenth century. Blacks were whipped, branded, put in shackles, and treated as property rather than as human beings. Sadly, many Christians used the Bible to defend slavery, and most others failed to speak up against it. Given this history and continuing challenges today, can you see why there is so much racial tension in our country?

Trap #2: Ignoring Progress Made on Race Relations

Another trap is to ignore the progress that has been made on race relations. There are Black icons and role models in every sector of American life, including education, politics, sports, music, business, Hollywood, and law, to name a few. Radio host Dennis Prager has raised five arguments against the claim that America is a racist country. You may disagree with him, but they're worth taking seriously.[4] For instance, he asks why there are so many race hoaxes if racism is entrenched in America? In his book *Hate Crime Hoax*, Wilfred Reilly examines over one hundred cases of alleged hate crimes that turn out to be hoaxes. Yes, hate crimes exist. But if America is so racist, asks Prager, why are people inventing so many hate crimes?

And further, why would *millions* of Blacks from Africa and the Caribbean voluntarily immigrate to the United States today if racism is so deeply entrenched in our country? (Interestingly, Nigerians are among the most successful immigrant communities.)

Great progress has been made in America, but much work

remains to be done. Honesty compels us to keep both of these ideas in tension.

What Can We Do?

Here are a few actions steps:

1. *Build relationships with people of different ethnicities.* It is easy, and natural, to make friends with people who are like you. Be different. Reach out to people of different races and get to know them as friends. Be eager to hear and learn about their life experiences.

2. *Root out racism in your own heart.* Regardless of our skin color, we are all susceptible to developing racist beliefs about others. The Bible makes it clear that *no one* is righteous (see Romans 3:10). That includes you and me. Thus, we will never be able to move beyond racial hostilities unless we *each* humbly recognize our own shortcomings and need for forgiveness. It is easy to become defensive when charges of racism are thrown around so flippantly and consistently. Yet Christians of every race must be willing to examine their own blind spots.

3. *Be a good listener.* Whether in books, YouTube videos, blogs, or conversations, seek out different voices on issues of race and listen well to their perspectives. My father has often said to me, "It is more important

to understand than to be understood." Especially on issues of race, choose to understand where others are coming from by listening to their points of view. As James said, "Be quick to hear, slow to speak" (James 1:19).

PART 4

Sexuality

15

Sex

THERE IS A SEXUAL REVOLUTION going on among your generation. But despite what the media might say, this is not a sexual revolution against traditional values like what happened in the 1960s. In that era, it was countercultural to have sex before marriage, to watch pornography, or to enter into an LGBTQ relationship. Today, these have become commonplace.

The real revolution today is the many young people who are choosing to follow Jesus rather than to accept the cultural script of sex, love, and relationships. The real revolution is young people like *you*, who are sick and tired of being bombarded with false information about sex and who want to know how to love God and their neighbors with their sexuality.

I am convinced that your generation wants real answers about sex. But I'm also not naive. Because you are growing up in such a sex-saturated culture, you have more hurdles to overcome to follow Jesus than any generation in modern history. You can hardly browse the Internet, watch YouTube, enter social media, or walk down the street without getting bombarded with a counterfeit message about sex.

In such a world, who can possibly expect you to follow God's design for relationships? The answer is simple: *God can*. His standards haven't changed, even if our culture's have. I understand the incredible challenges you face in this arena, but you are capable of doing the right thing. God will "equip you with everything good that you may do his will" (Hebrews 13:21).

The Heart of the Question

Have you ever wondered why God gave the specific command not to eat the fruit of one specific tree in the Garden of Eden? Why *that* command? After all, fruit is made to be eaten and enjoyed, and Adam and Eve could eat all the other fruit in the Garden. And this fruit looked tasty to the senses, striking to the eyes, and appealing to the mind (see Genesis 3:6). Why didn't God say to Adam, "You can do anything in the Garden, but don't murder Eve"? Given how excited he was to first see her, this command would have been so much easier to follow!

My friend Rachel Gilson said it best: "What is the motivation to obey a law that seems nonsensical? It can only be deep trust in the one who asks."[1] Obeying a law against murder doesn't require trust. It's obvious that we shouldn't kill people. But God wasn't interested in creating human beings just to follow laws. God created us to be in relationship with one another and with him. And since he is the Creator and we are not, we are going to have to trust him, *even when things don't make sense to us.*

In the Garden of Eden, Satan tempted Adam and Eve by trying to undermine their confidence in God's character. Did God really have their best interest in mind, or was he keeping them from all the fun? They didn't understand *why* God commanded them not to eat the fruit, and so they chose to rebel.

Aren't we faced with the same kind of choice today? The world offers "fruit" that looks pleasurable, fun, and satisfying. It is as if Satan were saying, "Is sexual activity really that big of a deal? Does porn really hurt anyone? As long as sex is consensual, there's nothing wrong with it, right? Are you really going to judge someone else for how they love? Why embrace a view of sex, love, and gender that seems so closed-minded? Isn't the Christian sexual ethic unrealistic today?"

God's Commandments Are for Your Good

The biggest reason I trust God is because of Jesus. Jesus reveals God's character through his tender kindness for those caught in the snare of sin, his compassion for the sick and demon-possessed, and his willingness to lay down his life for our salvation. If you want to know what God is like, look at Jesus. He lived the most loving, gracious, and beautiful life *ever*.

Not only is God good, but his commands are for our good. King David said he loved the law of the Lord (see Psalm 119:97). And before the Israelites entered the Promised Land, Moses gave commandments to the people that were intended for their good (see Deuteronomy 10:12-13). Jesus said following his commands would bring joy (see John 15:10-11). We may not understand all God's commandments about sex, but the biggest question is *Will we trust him?*

We might not always understand why following God's commands is best for us. But consider this: What would the world be like if everyone followed God's plan for sex and the family? Would the world be better or worse? The answer is obvious:

- There would be no sexual exploitation, sexual trafficking, or sexual abuse.
- There would be no sexually transmitted diseases.
- There would be no crude, degrading sexual humor.
- There would be no pain from divorce.
- There would be no deadbeat dads.
- Kids would be brought into families with a mom and a dad who love each other.

Seriously, wouldn't such a world be far better than our own? Of course!

God's Design Brings Freedom

We often think of rules as restrictive, but although it may strike you as counterintuitive, following God's plan for sex will actually make you *more* free. How so? Let me explain.

One of my friends took his junior high youth group to play paintball. On the way home, a seventh grader announced to his friends that he loved it so much that someday he wanted to be in the military and go to war.

An older youth worker who had been to war spoke up and said, "You are missing the point. Paintball is fun because there are no consequences. You might get hit with a paintball, and at most you will have a welt. In paintball, you are free to play the game without inhibitions because there is no fear of lasting consequences. But in war, there are extreme consequences, and there is great fear. If you get hit with a bullet, it might cost you your life."

Sex within marriage is not unlike playing a game of paintball in one key sense: you are free to enjoy yourself without fear of negative consequences. Following God's plan for sex enables couples to not worry about rejection, comparison, contracting an STD, or a broken condom. God's plans are not meant to steal our fun but to help us flourish in our relationships with others.

There is so much confusion over the nature of freedom today. An alcoholic once said to me, "I am free to drink if I like." I replied, "Are you free *not* to drink for a day?" He was silent. Many young people today think they are free to do whatever they want sexually as long as there is consent and no one gets hurt. But this is not true freedom. Real freedom is having the capacity to live as God designed you to live, *regardless of how you feel.* Just like a smartphone that is designed to function a certain way, God designed you and me for a purpose. We only experience real freedom when we follow the loving plan of our Creator.

Does this mean that people who reject God's design don't enjoy sex? Of course not. The prodigal son seemed to enjoy living in sin for a season before he "came to himself" (Luke 15:17). My point is not that you should obey God's commandments because it will benefit you. Paul does not say to the Corinthian church, "Avoid sexual immorality because God's plan is the road to the best sex." As we have seen, God's commands *are* for our good, and we are designed to flourish when we embrace them. But this is not the *motivation* for sexual purity. The motivation for being sexually pure should be to honor God with our bodies. Our motivation is to be holy because *God* is holy. Our motivation is to honor God.

What Is the Purpose of Sex?

If freedom comes from living as God has designed us to live, then what is his purpose for sex? The Bible gives three main purposes.

1. *Procreation:* Quite obviously, sex is about making babies. Genesis 1:28 makes this clear. Being fruitful

and multiplying on the earth is both a command and a blessing.

2. *Unity:* One of the most powerful aspects of sex is its ability to bond people together. Genesis 2:24 says, "A man shall leave his father and his mother and hold fast to his wife, and they shall become one flesh." When a couple has sex, something changes in their relationship. They have entered into a deeper, "one flesh" union that is not only spiritual but also emotional, relational, and even biochemical (which is one reason it is especially difficult for teenagers to break up after they have been sexually active).

3. *Foreshadowing heaven:* The Bible begins with a wedding between Adam and Eve (see Genesis 2). The apostle Paul tells us that marriage has existed since Creation to point us to the mysterious union between Christ and the church (see Ephesians 5:31-32). Human history even culminates with the "marriage of the Lamb" (Revelation 19:7), which is the heavenly wedding of Christ (the groom) and the church (the bride).

Why is this so important? Christopher West notes, "The union of the sexes—as beautiful and wonderful as it is in the divine plan—is only a faint glimmer, a pale picture within time of the eternal union with God."[2] When people focus merely on the physical element of sex and ignore the relational, spiritual, and emotional dimensions, they miss the deeper unity—the intimate connection—that occurs between two people in the act of sex. It is *this* kind of holistic union that foreshadows the kind of *greater* union we will have with God and others in heaven.

The cultural obsession with sex today misses its deeper purpose of foreshadowing our union with God in heaven. Since our culture has lost the transcendent meaning of sex and focuses merely on the physical, many people today think that sex itself is the route to happiness. Thus, rather than worshiping the Creator, people today worship the created thing (sex). The Bible calls this idolatry (see Romans 1:18-32).

Here is something else our culture desperately misses: *even the most wonderful sex life cannot satisfy the craving of the human heart for love and connection.* I have been married to my wife for over two decades. I thank God for my caring, loving, and beautiful bride. Yet she is not my ultimate fulfillment, and I am not hers. We both know that any human relationship—including our own—cannot ultimately fulfill the deepest yearning of our hearts for love and relationship.

Sex is beautiful. But remember, it is foreshadowing the deep intimacy we will experience with God and others in heaven. This doesn't mean that heaven involves endless sexual bliss (as some religions describe it). It simply means that sexual union on earth is a pointer, an anticipation, a foreshadowing of a *deeper* union we will all experience in heaven.

Standing Boldly for Sexual Purity

Here are three quick tips for following God's design for sex.

1. *Avoid sexually tempting situations.* The Bible tells believers to resist Satan and to "flee from sexual immorality" (1 Corinthians 6:18). Whether it is avoiding parties, certain social media apps, or being on your phone when you are alone, the wise Christian thinks about sexually tempting situations *ahead of time* and avoids them.

2. *Have an accountability structure.* Whether it's a parent, youth pastor, teacher, or friend, we all need someone to ask us the tough questions about our sexual choices, to show us grace when we fail, and to help keep us accountable.

3. *Experience God's grace.* None of us can stand totally pure before God. We have all fallen short. But the good news is that God forgives us. Let me state it clearly: *no matter what you have done, or what has been done to you, God forgives you.* Like the father of the Prodigal Son, God yearns for you to experience his love and forgiveness. Don't let your past determine your future. God loves *you.*

Homosexuality

As an atheist with same-sex attraction, Rachel never thought she would end up becoming a follower of Jesus. But to her own surprise, it happened.

Her faith journey began in a philosophy class at Yale University. Her professor presented an argument for the existence of God that she rejected, but it made her wonder if there were *better* arguments she should consider. And so she began to research further.

Wanting to know if God was okay with same-sex unions, Rachel asked one of the few Christians she knew at Yale for some guidance. Interestingly, this girl was a lesbian and believed that God was fine with same-sex romantic relationships. She gave Rachel some material to read. Even though Rachel had no formal biblical training, she was not convinced. Looking at the biblical passages in context (as we will do below) made it very clear that God had designed sex to be experienced in the marital union of one man and one woman. Rachel knew that if she became a Christian, it meant saying no to same-sex romance.

To make a long story short, Rachel stole a copy of C. S. Lewis's *Mere Christianity* from a friend, read it carefully, and became a Christian.

God began to change her life radically, but some nagging questions persisted: *What should I do with my same-sex attraction? Why would God not want me to act on the desire for love? If it felt so right to be attracted to the same sex, how could it be condemned as wrong?* What made it especially hard was the incessant cultural message to follow her sexual desires. She had also had a few girlfriends, so the issue was very personal for her.

Rachel quickly understood what the Bible teaches about same-sex unions, but she struggled to understand why. Yet as she wrestled with the issue more deeply, the most pressing question in her mind became *Will I obey God, even if I don't understand?*

This is the heart of the issue.

Following a "Nonsensical" Law

As we saw in the last chapter, there is one good reason for following a law even if we don't understand it: *trust in the one who gave it*. While it seemed that God was withholding something

good from her—like with Adam and Eve in the Garden—
Rachel ultimately decided that God could be trusted with her
sexuality. Why? The answer is simple: Jesus. "Yes," she said,
"I could trust God because in Christ he had proven himself
trustworthy."[1] She found his love sweeter, richer, and more
beautiful than anything the world has to offer.

Although it may surprise you, Rachel is now happily married to a man and is a mother. Looking back, she can see why
God designed sex for marriage. Sex is what brings children
into the world, and they thrive best with both a mom and a
dad. And marriage is meant to depict God's relationship with
the church, which requires the difference between male and
female to illustrate God's great love for humankind.

There is much more to her story than this.[2] Yet here's the
key point I hope you take away: though they don't get much
attention from the wider culture, there are many Christians
with same-sex attractions who are being faithful to the sexual
ethic of Jesus, and they are experiencing rich lives. Some are
living faithfully in marriage, and others are living faithfully
as singles. To counter many of the false narratives in our
culture, and to give people hope, their stories *need* to be told.

Can You Be Gay and Christian?

How we might answer this question depends on what we
mean by "gay." Let's consider three different ways this question can be taken.

First, can a Christian experience same-sex attraction? Of

course. Many Christians do. Many of my Christian friends have shared with me that this is a continuing struggle for them. Same-sex attraction doesn't magically disappear when someone chooses to follow Jesus. As Christians, we can experience all sorts of attractions that are not in line with how God wants us to live.

Second, can a Christian commit sexual sin, including engaging in homosexual behavior, and be forgiven? Absolutely! Engaging in homosexual behavior is *not* the unforgivable sin. The Bible does take same-sex sexual behavior seriously, as it does all forms of sexual sin, but the Bible also says, "If we confess our sins, [Jesus] is faithful and just to forgive us our sins and to cleanse us from all unrighteousness" (1 John 1:9). In case you missed it, the word *all* means *ALL*.

Third, can a person engage in unrepentant same-sex sexual behavior and be a Christian? That's tougher to answer. The Bible is *clear* that sex is meant for one man and one woman in marriage. Also, the apostle Paul places homosexual behavior in the category of sins that keep someone from inheriting the Kingdom of God (see 1 Corinthians 6:9-11). While God ultimately judges the heart, practicing homosexual behavior violates God's desire for the Christian life. It is something God calls us away from and not toward.

What the Bible Says about Same-Sex Sexual Behavior

The Bible has much to say about homosexual behavior, but for brevity and clarity, we can ask two important questions to start us off.

What Did Jesus Think?

To understand what Scripture teaches about homosexual behavior, it is first necessary to understand God's original blueprint for human sexuality. As we saw in the last chapter, God designed sex to be experienced only within the marital union of one man and one woman (see Genesis 1–2). When asked about the permissibility of divorce, Jesus affirmed this Creation account as the standard for human relationships (see Matthew 19:3-6). Although Jesus did not mention homosexual behavior explicitly in his teaching, he condemned all sexual behavior outside the marriage relationship (see, for example, Mark 7:21-22), which would include both heterosexual and homosexual behavior. To put it simply, Jesus believed that same-sex sexual behavior violated God's design for sexuality.

What Did Paul Think?

The apostle Paul, under the inspiration of the Holy Spirit, wrote much of the New Testament and is one of the primary sources in teaching us how to think Christianly about any issue. In Romans 1:21-27, Paul explains that just as turning to idols violates our rightful duty to worship our Creator, turning to same-sex sexual relations violates God's natural design for the use of our bodies. Some have claimed that Paul was only condemning pederasty, a socially permissible sexual relationship between a man and a boy that was prevalent in ancient Greece. However, in this passage, Paul describes the men as performing the same kind of unnatural practice as the women, yet there was no female practice of pederasty. Thus, Paul cannot be speaking just about pederasty in Romans 1.

Others have claimed that Paul was condemning excessive lust, not loving same-sex relationships. In this passage, Paul *does* say that people were "consumed with passion for one another." But he also condemns the acts themselves. Why? Because they reflect a denial of the existence of God by violating his clearly seen design for men and women (see 1:18-21). The focus of Romans 1 is not on excessive lust but on the idolatrous nature of people who have suppressed their knowledge of God, worshiping things in creation rather than the Creator and rejecting God's natural design for sexual relations. As with Jesus, Paul points *back* to Creation to ground sexual morality.

Other biblical passages address homosexual behavior, such as Leviticus 18:22 and 1 Corinthians 6:9. We are just skimming the surface here. I hope you will read more on this topic so you can develop biblical convictions about God's design for sex.[3] Nevertheless, it should be clear that a straightforward reading of the Bible reveals that God has designed sex to be between one man and one woman in marriage.

How Should We Respond?

Allow me to offer three thoughts.

1. *If you are a Christian who experiences same-sex attraction, please know that you are not alone.* There are many

Christians, young and old, who understand. God loves you deeply. You are made in his image, and he yearns to be in relationship with you. Please know that God's grace extends to you—yes, *you*. You are loved.

2. *Be a good friend.* I recently met a Christian teenage girl who befriended a gay classmate who was an atheist. Rather than feeling the need to tell him he's living in sin, she simply aims to love him as God loves us—"while we were still sinners" (Romans 5:8). They talk, watch movies together, and just hang out. Yet when the topic comes up, she graciously shares her beliefs and points to Christ. She certainly hopes he will become a believer, but whether it happens or not, she cares about him as a friend and as an individual made in the image of God. Her approach is to be ready with an answer for her beliefs, and when the time arises, to share them with "gentleness and respect" (1 Peter 3:15). Who can you reach out to as a friend like this with the love of Jesus?

3. *Stay faithful to Scripture.* Some people today will tell you the Bible approves of same-sex sexual relationships. Others will call you a hateful bigot if you embrace God's design for sex and marriage. Don't believe it. As we saw in the example of Rachel Gilson, true freedom comes not from rejecting the teachings of Jesus but from trusting our lives to the One who made us and loves us.

17

Transgender Ideology

⚡

WHILE THE BIBLE IS THE BESTSELLING BOOK of all time, Harry Potter is the bestselling series ever. The author, J. K. Rowling, has been one of the most beloved authors on the planet for decades, but recently that began to change. She has received public criticism from fans and stars like Daniel Radcliffe and Emma Watson (who play characters in the Harry Potter films). People have accused her of hatred, called her vile names, and threatened her.

What did Rowling do to receive such ire? She challenged the transgender narrative.[1]

For both personal and professional reasons, Rowling began researching the topic of transgenderism extensively, which included spending time listening to the stories of transgender people and coming to care for them as individuals. Yet fully aware of the pending backlash, Rowling couldn't stay silent. She was too worried about trans activism not to speak up.

One of her big concerns is freedom of speech. Trans activists, she noted, are quick to silence (and punish) those who don't embrace their narrative, and some of their initiatives have been inching their way into law. Yet the primary motivator was that Rowling became concerned about certain groups of people who were experiencing negative effects because of trans activism. This group includes female prisoners, sex abuse survivors, and the growing number of young women who regret their decision to transition and are transitioning back to their original sex (detransitioners).

Rowling was also deeply troubled by the massive increase in young girls who are being referred to transitioning treatment. A few years ago, the majority of people who wanted to transition to the opposite sex were male. But now this group is overwhelmingly female. In the UK, where Rowling lives, the percentage of teenage girls seeking gender treatment has increased 4,400 percent.[2] A disproportionately high percentage of these girls are on the autism spectrum.[3]

After reading stories of people with gender dysphoria describing their experience of anxiety, eating disorders, and self-hatred, Rowling wondered if, had she been born thirty years later, she might have tried to transition. "The allure of escaping womanhood would have been huge," she said. "If

I'd found community and sympathy online that I couldn't find in my immediate environment, I believe I could have been persuaded to turn myself into the son my father had openly said he'd have preferred."

Can you grasp the depth of her pain?

The Transgender Craze

In her book *Irreversible Damage: The Transgender Craze Seducing Our Daughters*, Abigail Shrier explores the question of why there has been such an increase in young people—and especially adolescent girls—identifying as transgender. "We should begin," she says, "by noting that adolescent girls today are in a lot of pain."[4] Depression. Loneliness. Anxiety. Suicide. As we explored in earlier chapters, all of these phenomena have been rising among young people.

How does the pain in your generation relate to the growth of transgender identities? According to Shrier, a transgender identity offers freedom from anxiety, satisfies the need for belonging, and offers the thrill of rebellion.[5] Identifying as transgender is one way some young people aim to fulfill the deep human needs that we all share.

Are these the only reasons someone might identify as transgender? Of course not. Some describe experiencing gender dysphoria for as long as they can remember. The issues involved with the transgender phenomenon are complex and go far beyond our discussion here. The reason I started with the story of J. K. Rowling and focused on the phenomenon of rapid-onset gender dysphoria (ROGD) is so that you would see that there is far more to the story than you may typically hear.

Defining Terms

For clarity in this discussion, let's define our terms. *Transgender* refers to a person who experiences incongruence between their biological sex and their gender identity. Many transgender people describe their experience as feeling trapped in the wrong body.

Gender dysphoria describes the psychological distress that some transgender people experience. While most people with gender dysphoria identify as transgender, some don't. Not all transgender people experience gender dysphoria. Transgender is an identity; gender dysphoria is a *psychological* condition.

People who are *intersex* experience atypical development of their sexual anatomy or sex chromosomes. For instance, some intersex males have an unusually small penis. In a minor number of cases, some individuals have both XX and XY chromosomes, which can lead to the development of both male and female sex organs. Intersex is a *biological* condition.

Transgenderism is an *ideology* promoted by certain activists that aims to transform cultural understandings of sex and gender. The goal is to uproot the idea that humans are naturally sexed beings and to move society away from being shaped by the gender binary. Transgenderism is being pushed in the media[6] as well as in the educational system,[7] legal system, Hollywood, some churches, and so on.

J. K. Rowling is not alone in her questioning of transgender ideology. Along with Christians and many conservatives, there are lesbians, feminists, and medical professionals who are opposed to transgender ideology. Even a number of transsexuals who have had sex-change surgery are opposed to it.[8]

A Biblical View of Gender

A ton could be said about the Bible and gender, but for the sake of our discussion, three points are vital.

First, *sex is an essential part of what it means to be human.* God could have made three sexes, or he could have made us asexual, but he chose to make human beings male and female (see Genesis 1:27). Unlike height, socioeconomic status, or intelligence, biological sex is an *essential* part of what it means to be human. God made us sexed beings. Biological sex is a good part of God's creation and is a key part of who we are each made to be.

Second, *whenever the Bible addresses crossing gender boundaries, it does so critically.* This is true in both the Old Testament and the New Testament (see, for example, Deuteronomy 22:5; 1 Corinthians 11:2-16; Romans 1:26-27). While these passages do not address the modern transgender debate directly, they do strongly imply that there are differences between males and females and that we are to live in accordance with our biological sex.

Third, *the Bible allows some flexibility in how to live out our biological sex*. The Bible does not give universal, cross-cultural guidance for being male or female. God calls us to live in congruence with our biological sex, but we have to work out that principle within culture. Consider the example of Jacob and Esau. Esau was a hairy hunter. Jacob had smooth skin and was favored by his mother, Rebekah. Was Esau more manly and Jacob more feminine? According to certain stereotypes, we might say yes. But the Bible makes no such distinction. In fact, God chose Jacob as the father of Israel! It is a mistake to deny that males and females are unique. It is also a mistake to take certain cultural beliefs—such as hunting and being hairy—and make them universal. We must find a balance between respecting the biological sex God has given us without uncritically adopting certain cultural stereotypes.

Key Claims of Transgender Ideology

Transgender ideology is based on a few key claims. Let's consider three.

Claim #1: If You Don't Affirm Someone with Gender Dysphoria, They May Commit Suicide

This is a serious charge, but it raises a couple of questions. First, does gender dysphoria cause feelings of suicide? We have no good evidence that this is the case. People with gender dysphoria often suffer from a range of mental health problems that likely contribute to suicidal ideation. Second, is there good evidence that affirmation improves mental health? Again, the evidence is lacking. One long-term study showed a rise in suicidality after sex reassignment surgery. Another study failed to show improved mental health for girls who had taken puberty suppressors.[9] At the very least, these studies indicate there may be more to consider for those who make the claim that not affirming someone with gender dysphoria will lead to suicide.

Claim #2: Gender Identity Cannot Change

Why would trans activists be interested in arguing that gender identity doesn't change? The answer is so they can get the same protective rights as other groups based on immutable characteristics such as race and sex. However, far from gender identity being unchangeable, multiple studies have shown that roughly two-thirds of kids who experience gender dysphoria (and are not affirmed or socially transitioned) eventually revert to identifying with their biological sex.[10] This doesn't mean every person with gender dysphoria eventually experiences relief, but many do.

Claim #3: Medical Transition is Safe.

Trans activists often claim that transitioning is safe. But consider puberty blockers, for example, which temporarily suppress puberty. Some studies reveal a range of health risks.[11] Or consider testosterone, which can lift depression and make a young girl feel emboldened. But not only do serious aches and pains come along with testosterone; it can also raise the risk of heart disease, diabetes, stroke, cancer, and blood clots.[12] Also, if a girl stops taking it, her body cannot revert back to its natural feminine form.

Though these claims are often made and accepted, the numerous scientific studies cited above indicate that, at very least, we may need to reconsider their truthfulness and safety.

What Can We Do?

Consider three steps.

1. *Love your transgender friends.* Most individuals who are transgender are not activists. They want love, belonging, and happiness—the same things all of us want. Be a good friend. Treat them with kindness, as you would (hopefully) treat anyone else. First John 4:18 says that "perfect love casts out fear." Rather than being motivated by fear, choose to treat them lovingly. They are made in the image of God and deserve love and respect.

2. *Be quick to listen and slow to speak.* James, the half-brother of Jesus, said to be "quick to hear, slow to speak" (James 1:19). Rather than looking to "fix" people who are transgender, focus on being a good listener. Ask questions and show sincere interest in their life experiences. Listen, listen, listen.

3. *Speak truth compassionately.* Our culture promotes gender confusion. It punishes those who stray from the transgender narrative. Be willing to speak truth, but do so with kindness. Remember: standing for both truth and love will make you a rebel today. But be like the apostles of Jesus, who were more concerned with obeying God than seeking the praise of other people (see Acts 4:18-20; 5:29). Only the truth can set people free (see John 8:32).

18

Pornography

EVERY GENERATION HAS FACED sexual temptation. Don't believe me? Just read the Bible! From the earliest chapters in Genesis to the book of Revelation, we see people falling prey to various kinds of sexual immorality. Sexual temptation and brokenness are nothing new.

But compared with the history of the world, there are some radical shifts that have taken place in your generation. In particular, pornography has transformed how people think about sex, love, and relationships. Consider three ways porn is different today than in the past:

1. *Accessible:* In the past, porn was painted on cave walls, drawn in books, or put in magazines or movies. Your

generation is the first raised with unlimited access to porn *just one click away.* Mobile technology has made porn available anytime, anywhere.

2. *Acceptable:* Can you think of a show you have seen where people debate the morality of porn? I can't. They did in the past but rarely anymore. In one study, teens and young adults ranked not recycling as more immoral than viewing porn (56 percent vs. 32 percent).[1] In the eyes of many people, judging someone's use of porn is worse than actually viewing porn. Porn has become acceptable in society.

3. *Aggressive:* Today, porn is not just about nudity or people having sex. It is increasingly violent and contains physical aggression toward women, who often respond as if they enjoy the way they are being treated.

Like many things, increased technology has transformed porn into a completely different and far more dangerous issue today than it was a few short years ago.

What's the Big Deal?

You might be wondering why this is such a big deal. After all, isn't everyone watching it? It's just harmless entertainment, right? The answer is an unequivocal *no.* Consider the many victims of pornography.

Porn Hurts Actresses

Few people think about how porn stars are affected. After all, many give their consent. Former female performer Eden Alexander described the pain she received during one scene: "I've never received a beating like that before in my life. I have permanent scars up and down the backs of my thighs. It was all things that I had consented to, but I didn't know quite the brutality of what was about to happen to me until I was in it."[2]

She is not alone. Many female performers report similar abuse.[3] Some porn may be consensual. But as long as the industry exists, the women who are involved in it will continue to be abused.

Porn Affects the Audience

You might be tempted to think that porn doesn't affect *you*. If you think that way, is it possible you're wrong? I believe it harms you in three ways:

HARM #1: PORN HURTS YOUR SOUL

Years ago, I talked with a young man who was habitually looking at porn. After he opened up to me about his habit, I asked him a simple question: "How does it affect you?" I will never forget his tepid response: "I can't look at a woman without undressing her in my mind."

This young man is not alone in terms of having his worldview shaped by viewing porn. (And just to be clear, porn is an issue for males and females both.) A major study by a group of four researchers concluded that young people who look at porn are more likely to be sexually aggressive, have more permissive sexual attitudes, accept the notion of casual sex, engage in risky sexual behavior, engage in sexual harassment, and be clinically depressed.[4]

You might be thinking this study merely reveals correlation but not causation—that these things are related but not caused by porn. This is a fair caution to raise, but the research points beyond correlation alone. Consider loneliness. While lonely people are often drawn to pornography for relief, there is good reason to believe porn *fosters* feelings of loneliness and isolation. According to Dr. Grant Benner, in an article for *Psychology Today*, "Pornography use begets loneliness, and loneliness begets pornography use."[5] It's a two-way street.

HARM #2: PORN HURTS YOUR BELIEFS

Perhaps the best way to see how porn affects people is to consider the *script* of pornography. We all have scripts about how we are supposed to behave in different settings. We have a script about how to behave in an elevator (face forward and don't say much), which is different from the script of how to behave at a football game (cheer for your team and boo the referee for a bad call).

Most of us were not formally taught how to behave in an elevator or at a football game; we simply observed people and followed along. We have learned scripts about how to behave at church, in a library, at a concert, at the dinner table, and so on. Here's the pressing question: *Where did you learn your script about sex?* While I don't know your story, I know your generation has gotten much of its sexual script from porn.

Here's why this is so important: porn offers an unrealistic, exaggerated, and harmful script of sex. Porn portrays marital sex as boring but extramarital sex as exciting. It presents women not as individuals to be loved and cherished but as sex objects to be used by men for pleasure. Violent porn sends the message that women can be harmed *if* men enjoy it. No wonder so many girls feel pressure to perform oral sex on boys, engage in anal sex, or tolerate emotional or physical abuse from boys: they've been influenced by the porn script.

Hebrews 13:4 says, "Let marriage be held in honor among all, and let the marriage bed be undefiled, for God will judge the sexually immoral and adulterous." Sadly, porn *mocks* the institution of marriage and promotes a script that directly violates God's beautiful design for sexual relationships.

HARM #3: PORN HURTS YOUR BRAIN

When I was in elementary school, my father led a national campaign on sexual purity. After one of his lectures, a woman approached him for counsel. She shared how her husband could not be sexually intimate with her without having a pornographic magazine on the pillow next to her head. Heartbroken, she asked my father for advice.

Even though I was young, I remember feeling sad for her. Why did her husband "need" porn? The answer is revealing: he had rewired his brain through habitual porn use to respond sexually to *an image* of a person rather than to a *real* person. Sadly, he couldn't fully love his wife *as his wife was* without bringing pornography into their relationship. Can you imagine how demeaned she felt?

Few people realize how deeply porn rewires the brain and thus shapes human behavior. The younger someone is, the more looking at porn shapes the development of his or her brain, which can have a lifelong impact. Research shows that it is far easier to quit gambling, alcohol addiction, heroin, and cocaine than porn. Why? Because of what it does to your brain.[6]

Many people claim that porn is not a big deal. But it is. It is no exaggeration to say that it is wreaking havoc on individuals, marriages, and society. As a father, it both breaks my heart and angers me that my kids have to grow up in such a pornified world.

What Can We Do?

Consider a few practical tips for avoiding pornography's snare. As a father, I hope and pray you will take these to heart.

1. *If you struggle with porn, I urge you to talk with someone you know who cares.* You are not alone. In fact, far more people struggle with pornography than you may realize. Please talk with someone—a youth pastor, parent, teacher, or friend—who will listen to you and help you.

2. *Remember that God loves you.* Viewing pornography is *not* the unforgivable sin. If you struggle with porn, God, like the father of the Prodigal Son, wants you to experience his love and forgiveness. Confess your sin to God and believe that he loves you deeply, as Scripture teaches (see Luke 15:11-32).

3. *Realize that porn use often masks a deeper brokenness.* If you have past hurts, they could be fueling your habit. Remember, God designed us to experience healthy relationships with him *and* with other people. Pornography aims to fill the good desire God has given us with a "relational counterfeit." Addressing habitual porn use *must* begin with the goal of becoming relationally healthy through building intimate connections with God and other people.

4. *If you have seen the damage porn causes to your generation, then consider asking how you can make a difference.* Share this chapter with a friend. Post a video critical of porn on social media.[7] Give a talk in school on the harms of pornography. Or think even bigger. Think about working for an organization such as Fight the New Drug, which educates people on the harms of porn.[8] Since there is a link between pornography and sex trafficking, consider committing your life to helping the victims of sex trafficking. You can make a difference.

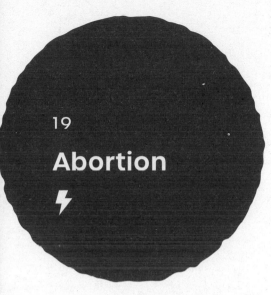

19

Abortion

⚡

THE ISSUE OF ABORTION IS NOT merely academic to me; it's *personal.* My youngest sister, Heather, was adopted into my family when she was just four weeks old. Even though I was only in fourth grade at the time, I will never forget the first time I held her as a newborn baby. Like all newborns, she weighed only a few pounds and was so precious and innocent. Now she is a beautiful wife and mother of three wonderful kids, my nephew and nieces.

Her birth mother was a young, unmarried teenager, totally unprepared to support a newborn. Years later, when Heather met her birth mother, she discovered that she had been conceived through rape. An older man forced her mother to have sex, and she became pregnant with Heather. Given her mother's unpreparedness, the forced pregnancy, and the shame that is often associated with young teen pregnancies, her mother could have easily chosen to have an abortion. But she didn't. She knew that every human life has value, regardless of how that life was conceived. Our family is grateful she chose life. We can't imagine our lives without Heather.

Quite obviously, not everyone chooses life. There have been *tens of millions* of abortions in the United States (and hundreds of millions worldwide) in recent times. As a result, many more people than you can imagine have had an experience with abortion. While not everyone who has had an abortion regrets it, many do. There are women who carry around the pain of having had an abortion and need to experience forgiveness. There are men who have encouraged their wives or girlfriends to have an abortion who need healing. There are many people who have been involved with and affected by abortion. If you have had an experience with abortion, please know that God forgives *you*.

As we attempt to consider this topic with grace and truth, let's remember: this issue involves every one of us. We can all be thankful our parents chose life, because if they hadn't, we wouldn't be here.

The Biblical Case for Life

The Bible never says, "Thou shalt not commit abortion." Why not? The main reason is that abortion would have been unimaginable to a Hebrew woman. Children were considered a gift from God (see Psalm 127:3). God was viewed as being sovereign over the womb (see Genesis 29:33; 1 Samuel 1:19-20). It was considered a curse to remain childless. The Bible is silent about abortion because it was *unthinkable* to the Hebrew mind.

Yet a simple case can be made that the Bible is pro-life.

First, *the Bible prohibits taking innocent human life.* The Ten Commandments condemn murder (see Exodus 20:13), and Jesus reaffirmed that human life should be protected (see, for example, Matthew 19:18).

Second, *the unborn is an innocent human being.* The same words are used in both the Old and New Testaments to describe the born and the unborn. In the Old Testament the Hebrew word *geber* was used to refer to a person at conception and a grown man (see Exodus 10:11; Deuteronomy 22:5; Judges 5:30; Job 3:3). In the New Testament, the word *brephos* is often used for unborn, newborn, and younger children (see Luke 1:41, 44; 18:15; 1 Peter 2:2). Scripture makes no relevant distinction between a preborn fetus and a newborn baby.

Therefore, the Bible is against abortion, which is taking the life of an innocent human being. Whether in the womb or out of the womb, the Bible condemns the unjust taking of innocent human life.

I've seen people argue on social media that the Bible is pro-choice, using Exodus 21:22-23, which discusses the penalty for men who struggle with one another and hit a pregnant woman. If the woman had a miscarriage, the argument goes, then the man would face a fine. But if one of the men killed the woman, then he would get the death penalty. Doesn't this prove the Bible values the unborn *less* than adults?

This is creative thinking, but it misses the point of the passage. For one, the word "miscarriage" is not used here. Proper interpretation indicates that the woman had a *premature* birth, not a miscarriage. The baby did not die in the process but was born early. Thus, the man should be fined. But if the mother *or* the unborn die, then the penalty is "life for life." Rather than undervaluing the life of the unborn, the passage considers it equal to the mother.[1]

The Bible unequivocally—in these passages as well as many others—prohibits abortion as the taking of an innocent human life.

But what does science say about this issue?

The Scientific Case for Life

Not long ago, I visited a pregnancy resource center. In touring the facility, I saw the piece of technology that convinces most pregnant women to choose life: the ultrasound machine. As soon as women are able to see a picture of the unborn baby inside them, they immediately realize it is a member of the human family. This intuition is supported by scientific data.

Consider the scientific case for pro-life.

First, *the unborn is alive.* People sometimes claim that we don't know when life begins, but scientifically speaking, there's no doubt. The mom is alive. The dad is alive. The sperm is alive. The egg is alive. The zygote is alive. There is no stage in the process of development when the unborn is not living.

Even if we didn't know when life began, we should still be against abortion. Why? Consider an example: If I were going to schedule a building for demolition but was unsure whether anyone was inside, should I proceed? Of course not! Former president Ronald Reagan said, "Anyone who doesn't feel sure whether we are talking about a second human life should clearly give life the benefit of the doubt. If you don't know whether a body is alive or dead, you would never bury it."[2] Even if there were uncertainty about when life begins, we should choose life. Nevertheless, we *do* know life begins at fertilization.

Second, *the unborn is separate from the mother.* The unborn may be dependent on the mother, but it is a distinct organism from the mother. We know this because the fetus has a unique DNA fingerprint, can have a different blood type from the mother, and if the parents are of different races, it can develop a different skin color from the mother.

And finally, *the unborn is human.* There is a simple way to know the unborn is human: consider the parents! Since beings reproduce after their kind, if we want to know what type of being an offspring is, ask a simple question: What type of parents did it have? If the parents are human, the offspring is human.

The science is clear: at fertilization, the unborn is a living, individual human being, separate from the mother.

The Philosophical Case for Life

Some pro-choice advocates point to differences between those in the womb and those outside the womb to deny the unborn the right to life. There *are* four key differences (which spell "SLED"), but none of these are significant enough to deny the right to life of the unborn.

S-Size: The unborn are clearly smaller than newborns. But does size have anything to do with the right to life? Is a basketball player more valuable than a gymnast? Just because the fetus is smaller than an adult does not mean it is not a valuable human being. In Dr. Seuss's *Horton Hears a Who*, Horton says, "A person's a person no matter how small." And that's certainly true in the abortion debate.

L-Level of Development: The unborn are less developed than newborns and adults. But this difference has no relevance to the essential nature of the unborn as human beings. Are adults more valuable than elementary children because they have gone through puberty? Are people with developmental disabilities less valuable than those without them? Human development begins at fertilization and continues throughout life.

E-Environment: The unborn lives in a different location than newborns and adults, but why is that relevant to its human nature? Do you stop being human when you change your location? How can *where* you are determine *what* you are?

D-Degree of Dependency: The unborn is fully dependent upon its mother for survival. But why does this make it a less valuable human being? If your humanity hinged upon how dependent you were, then what about toddlers, the disabled, or those on dialysis machines?

So much more could be said, but one thing should be clear: despite abortion's prevalence in the world, Scripture, science, and philosophy agree that the unborn being is a valuable human being from the moment of fertilization.

What Should I Do?

In college, Stephanie Gray Connors was planning to be an actress, but a pro-life speaker came to her college and pointed out that more people work to kill unborn babies than work to save them. It rocked her. Now she is a pro-life author and speaker. She was even invited to speak on abortion at Google.[5]

You, too, can make a difference, and there are many ways to do so. Share this chapter with a friend. Make a social media post defending life. Visit a pregnancy resource center. Support pro-life causes. Here's the bottom line: the unborn cannot speak up for themselves. Will *you* speak up for them?

Please allow me one final word of encouragement: *if you have had an abortion, God loves you and forgives you.* Abortion is not the unforgivable sin. Jesus died on the cross for all our sins, and like the father of the prodigal son, he is eager to forgive and embrace you if you are willing to come to him. Many women have had abortions and experienced God's loving forgiveness. If this is you, please share your experience with a trusted leader. Freedom awaits.

PART 5

Ethics

20

The
Environment

⚡

SEA LEVELS ARE RISING. Polar bears are dying. Air is becoming increasingly polluted. Floods, fires, droughts, and storms are increasing at unprecedented rates. If we don't make drastic changes in our approach to the climate, billions of people will die and civilization will likely end within a decade. According to student activist Greta Thunberg, climate change warrants a radical response: "I don't want you to be hopeful. I want you to panic. . . . I want you to act as you would in a crisis. I want you to act as if our house is on fire. Because it is."[1]

Does this doomsday scenario concern you? There's a decent chance it might. After all, your generation cites climate change as *the* most important issue facing the world today.[2]

Quite obviously, what you think about climate change has huge implications for your daily life. If the world is going to end within a decade, then many of you reading this won't even make it to your thirties! You probably won't get married. You certainly won't have grandkids. If we are really causing irreversible damage to the environment and the world is ending within a decade, then why plan for the future? Live for the moment! Furthermore, should we be surprised that there is an increase in depression and anxiety when your generation is told the world is ending soon?

Caring for the environment we live in is not an unimportant issue, and we must think about it carefully. But as we approach it, let's begin by pointing out two positions in the climate change debate we'd be wise to avoid.

Climate Change Alarmism

The bleak picture offered above is a good example of what we can call *climate alarmism*, and fortunately, there is good reason to question it. Facts have to be twisted to support the narrative that "our house is on fire," as Thunberg claims. Consider a few examples that undermine this doomsday narrative:

- *California fires:* Is climate change the primary factor for increased fires in California? The story is not that simple. While climate change may play a role, human behavior—such as population increase and forestry development—is statistically more significant.[3] What that means is that even if there is slight change in the California climate, the key reason for increased fires is not the climate change itself (whatever the cause may be) but how humans have, and have *not*, responded.

- *Polar bears: National Geographic* created a now-famous video of an emaciated, dying polar bear set to sad music. The caption read, "This is what climate change looks like." In reality, claims that polar bear populations would radically diminish have not materialized, and some climate alarmists have admitted this.[4]

- *Whales:* Despite common perceptions and claims, no species of whales is at risk of extinction. The whale population has increased substantially over the past few decades.[5]

Climate alarmism is nothing new. As a kid, I remember reports that the world was entering another ice age. Now we hear about global *warming*! The United Nations released a report that said governments "have a ten-year window of opportunity to solve the greenhouse effects before it goes beyond human control."[6] When did the UN release this report? *1989.*

Don't believe climate alarmists. The world is not ending soon because of climate change.

Climate Change Denial

Does this mean we shouldn't be concerned about climate change or the environment? Absolutely not! On the opposite side of climate alarmism is *climate change denial*. There is no debate that Earth's climate has naturally changed throughout its history, and sometimes dramatically. Scientists are increasingly confident that climate change occurs today and that humans are playing a role. The important questions they're asking have to do with the *amount* humans contribute to climate change and what kinds of measures, if any, we should take to lessen it.

Apart from climate change alarmism and climate change denial, thoughtful Christians can take different positions on the causes, effects, and solutions to climate change. While we may disagree over the details, all Christians should agree that we should care for creation and be willing to follow the truth wherever it leads.

God's Mandate: Care for Creation

Genesis 1–2 tells us that God created the world (1:1), called it good (1:31), and put humans in charge of stewarding it (1:26-30). Stewardship involves delighting in God's creation but also protecting, preserving, and ruling over what God has made. It involves harvesting crops, building roads for transportation, cutting down trees to make homes, and making things like clothes and smartphones. One way we love God is by caring for his beautiful creation, and we love our neighbors by protecting the environment that we all inhabit.

In the Sermon on the Mount, Jesus taught that God feeds the birds of the air and clothes the lilies of the field. He taught that the lilies are more beautiful than Solomon in "all his glory" (Matthew 6:28-29). If God cares about these things and delights in the beauty of creation, shouldn't we?

Animals matter to God too. Adam named the animals as part of his authority over them but also as a recognition that humans should care for them. Deuteronomy 5:14 says to give livestock a rest on the Sabbath because it is part of caring for *them*. Proverbs 12:10 says, "Whoever is righteous has regard for the life of his beast."

Some Christians are reluctant to embrace creation care. If God is going to return in judgment, and the Earth will be destroyed, what's the point? Some cite 2 Peter 3:10 in support of this view, which seems to indicate that on his return, Jesus will "burn" and "dissolve" heavenly bodies, and the Earth will be "done."

But two things can be said in response. First, even if God *is* going to destroy Earth in a future judgment, it doesn't follow that we shouldn't care for it *now*. Our physical bodies will decay and die someday, but does that mean we can abuse them in the present? Of course not. Second, it is likely that Peter is not referring to the physical Earth being destroyed but to the sinful world order we live in. God is going to destroy the evil that pervades our world, not the world itself.[7]

Avoiding Two Worldview Mistakes

A biblical view of creation helps us avoid two worldview mistakes. The first is to adopt *deism*, which is the view that God created the world but is not involved in it anymore. The Bible portrays God as being deeply involved with the world. Psalm 104 describes God making springs gush forth in the valleys, causing the grass to grow, and planting trees.

The second mistake is to adopt *pantheism*, which views everything as part of the divine. Pantheists see "God" and the universe as one. This often leads to treating trees and plants as sacred and worshiping "Mother Earth." In Genesis 1:1, God *speaks* creation into existence. God and creation are separate. Look at this simple chart that portrays how much greater God is than creation:

GOD	CREATION
Uncreated	Created
Eternal	Temporal
Self-existent	Dependent
Infinite	Finite
Uncaused	Caused

Worshiping creation rather than the Creator is not only foolish—it's idolatry.

The Religion of Apocalyptic Environmentalism

There are certainly many people who have accepted doom-and-gloom scenarios about the climate. The media deserves some of the blame, as do politicians.

But I believe there's a bigger reason: *environmentalism, and especially climate hysteria, acts as a religion for many people.* According to Michael Shellenberger, "apocalyptic environmentalism" has replaced traditional religion in the West. In the Christian tradition, humans have failed to be in proper relationship with God. In apocalyptic environmentalism, humans have failed to be in proper relationship with nature. Rather than looking to priests to interpret Scripture, apocalyptic environmentalists look to scientists to "interpret" nature. Recycling has replaced Communion as a "spiritual" practice. Rather than yearning for heaven, where we will be at peace with God and others, apocalyptic environmentalists encourage us to yearn for a future state when we are at peace with nature. Shellenberger explains:

> Apocalyptic environmentalism gives people a purpose: to save the world from climate change, or some other environmental disaster. It provides people with a story that casts them as heroes, which some scholars . . . believe we need in order to find meaning in our lives.[8]

I believe he's right. From what I've seen, worldview issues are often at the heart of climate debates.

What Can We Do?

Here are three quick things Christians can do:

1. *Be careful not to be taken by bad ideas or bad science.* Examine both sides, ask deep questions, and follow the truth wherever it leads. Avoid the positions of climate change alarmism *and* climate change denial. Be intentional about applying your Christian faith to how you think about the environment.

2. *In obedience to God, care for the environment.* Even a small thing, like picking up trash, is a way of loving your neighbor.

3. *Consider a life profession that aims to care for creation.* If you want to be a politician, help pass legislation that genuinely protects nature. If you want to be a scientist, create new technology that protects the environment. If you want to be a filmmaker, tell stories that capture the beauty of nature and encourage creation care.

21

Poverty

A FEW YEARS AGO, my friend Dan called me and asked if we could meet over coffee. He was leaving his comfortable pastoral position at a beach community in Southern California to work at the Union Rescue Mission in Los Angeles, which is in the heart of Skid Row.

Why would he voluntarily leave such a comfortable, safe, and stress-free environment to work in one of the poorest and most broken places in America? Most people want to make more money and *avoid* difficulty. Yet Dan was going to make less money and have a more stressful life! Why?

The simple answer is that God changed his heart. There's certainly nothing wrong with working as a pastor in a beautiful beach community. People in wealthy communities, as all people, need pastors to care for them. But when Dan studied the scriptural command to care for the poor, he became increasingly uncomfortable with his comfortable life.

The Bible and the Poor

The Bible has a lot to say about the subject of poverty. In both the Old and New Testaments, wealthy people are judged harshly for disregarding the needs of the poor. In the Old Testament, the prophet Amos condemns wealthy women "who oppress the poor, who crush the needy" (Amos 4:1). When the Israelites reaped the harvest of their fields, they were commanded not to strip their vineyards bare or to gather fallen grapes. The reason was simple: "You shall leave them for the poor and for the sojourner" (Leviticus 19:10). Although we relate to God differently now that Jesus has come, this passage reveals God's heart for the poor.

In the New Testament, James, the brother of Jesus, scolded believers who dishonored the poor by treating them worse than the rich (see James 2:1-7). The Bible has a *ton* to say about how we are supposed to treat the poor.

To further the point, consider nine biblical principles:

1. Make provision for the poor (see Leviticus 19:9-10).
2. Treat the poor justly (see Leviticus 19:15).
3. Help the poor (see Leviticus 25:35-36).
4. Defend the rights of the poor (see Psalm 82:3-4).

5. Be generous to the poor (see Proverbs 14:21).
6. Do not oppress the poor (see Proverbs 14:31).
7. Hear the cries of the poor (see Proverbs 21:13).
8. Serve the poor and treat them with honor (see Luke 14:12-14).
9. Do not discriminate against the poor (see James 2:2-4).

Quite obviously, God values the poor! He was furious with Israel when they failed to care for the poor and oppressed. As followers of Jesus, it is part of our job description to defend, love, and provide for the poor (see Matthew 25:31-46).

Not long ago, I brought a group of high school students to work with Dan at the Union Rescue Mission for a few days. The students served meals in the kitchen, played Bingo with mission residents, cleaned, played with children, served cold water to people living on the streets, shared meals with strangers, and slept on the roof of the mission. The trip was transformative for both the students and me, and we hope it was for some of the people we encountered.

During our visit, and in my study since, it has become clear that Christians tend to have some *huge* misconceptions about poverty.

Misconception #1: Poverty Is about a Lack of Money

Perhaps the biggest misconception is that poverty is primarily about a lack of having *things*. In their book *When Helping*

Hurts, Steve Corbett and Brian Fikkert observe, "North American Christians need to overcome the materialism of Western culture and see poverty in more relational terms."[1]

Think about it: When you hear of people in poverty, do you tend to focus on physical things they lack, such as food, clothes, running water, housing, and medicine? Or do you think in terms of shame, powerlessness, depression, and hopelessness, which are what low-income people often feel? Chances are you think in material terms. But is lacking material goods at the heart of poverty?

What if poverty is more complex than merely lacking *things*? For instance, African American scholar Cornel West believes the basic issue behind ghetto poverty is a "profound sense of psychological depression, personal worthlessness, and social despair" in Black America today.[2] While there is an economic dimension to poverty in the ghettos, according to West, the feelings of despair and hopelessness are core factors as well.

Ultimately, poverty stems not just from a lack of things but from broken relationships with God, others, and the self. Thus, if we want to address poverty, we have to be willing to help people cultivate a proper understanding of their own worth *and* develop healthy relationships with God and others. When people have healthy relationships, they are in a better position to experience the dignity that comes from working and supporting themselves and their families.

Can you see why effective help for the poor must involve more than simply meeting their material needs? The Union

Rescue Mission offers people food, shelter, clothes, and safety. But they also offer people life skills and opportunities to build relationships with others so they can develop as whole people.

Misconception #2:
Good Intentions Are Enough

There is another huge misconception about poverty: *good intentions are enough*. People often have the right motives to help the poor, but their methods end up bringing harm. The right desire to help the poor is, for example, what motivates many people to embrace socialism, the form of government in which society as a whole owns the means of production. Like the legend of Robin Hood, socialist politicians promise to redistribute wealth to the needy.

As appealing as socialism may sound, such systems have consistently failed to actually help the poor and, in many cases, have harmed them. Paul Copan observes, "The only cases where the world's masses have escaped grinding poverty—most accurately measured by increased income *per person*—is through the twin conditions of free markets and the enforcement of the rule of law."[3] Even though capitalism has flaws, it is the best system for helping masses of people escape poverty. Socialism consistently fails in this regard.

The misconception about good intentions also applies on a personal level. Should you give to a person asking for money? Personally, I often do two things when I see someone asking for money. First, I stop and talk to the person. I want them to know I see them and care. Second, while I rarely give money, I often offer to buy the person a drink or a meal. And if I have time and they are open to it, I might sit down and enjoy the meal with them.

What Can You Do?

Consider three ways you can help those in poverty.

1. *Don't buy the lie that the purpose of life is to get things.* Our culture promises happiness to those who have the right shoes, car, home, and so on. But this pursuit leads to emptiness. If poverty is not merely *lacking* material things, then richness is not merely *having* material things. The "rich" life is one that consists of meaningful relationships with God and other people that are focused on building God's Kingdom.

2. *Be grateful for what you have.* Since you are reading this book, you probably have more to be thankful for than you realize. You most likely have adults who care about you, a roof over your head, and your basic needs met. Have you ever thanked God for these things? The apostle Paul says to "give thanks in all circumstances" (1 Thessalonians 5:18). Why? At least one reason is that being grateful for what we have can help motivate us to be more generous with others.

3. *Be generous with others.* On our trip to Skid Row, Pastor Dan and I walked into downtown LA. We met

an older man who had formerly served in the US government but now lives on the streets and begs for a living. While he could get government aid, he feels that the government abandoned him at his point of greatest need, so he refuses their handouts. Instead, he gets about eight to ten dollars per day through begging.

Three people put money in his jar during our ten-minute conversation. Many people in expensive suits simply walked by as if he weren't even there. But the people who gave were others who were struggling as well. In other words, *the people who helped him the most were the people who seemingly had the least.* One man even handed him seven cents and said, "I hope it helps at least some. It's all I have."

I was reminded of the story Jesus told about the widow who put two small copper coins in the Temple offering box after the rich people put in large sums of money. Jesus praised her for giving out of her poverty, whereas the rich people gave out of their abundance (see Mark 12:43-44). After our conversation, Dan bought the man groceries and delivered them to him personally. That's how you make a difference.

22

Guns & Violence

⚡

I HAVE A CONFESSION TO MAKE. I could probably count on one hand the number of times I have shot a gun. I've been skeet shooting a few times. I've never been hunting. For my son's thirteenth birthday, I took him and his cousins to gun safety training, and then we shot pistols.

You might be wondering why I am sharing this. Doesn't this make me *lose* credibility on the issue of guns? That's possible. But I see it differently. Here's why: I don't feel the need to defend a particular issue related to guns. I'm not in the military or police force. I have not had a bad experience with guns, nor did I grow up with any animosity toward them. I simply want to know how Christians should think about questions that often relate to guns, such as these: Is it ever okay for a follower of Jesus to take another person's life, and if so, when? How do I balance the command to love my enemies with a readiness to act in my or others' defense?

These are tough questions that divide Christians. Whether you rarely shoot guns (like me) or regularly shoot them, your generation has been deeply shaped by the reality of gun violence. Movies, song lyrics, social media, and video games often glorify violence. Firearm-related injuries are among the leading causes of death among teens.[1] And even though school shootings account for 0.2 percent of annual gun deaths in the United States, nearly all schools have active shooter drills, which may contribute to increased fear and anxiety around the issue of guns.[2]

Let's step back from some of the emotion surrounding this issue and try to think clearly about God and guns.

The Heart of the Gun Debate

My guess is that you have no problem with someone owning a knife and probably not a shotgun or rifle either, but what about a tank? As cool as it might feel to drive a tank to school, my guess is that you probably think it's a bad idea for citizens to be able to own vehicles designed for mass destruction. Assuming that's your position, I totally agree!

Most of the modern debate about gun ownership is not *if* people should be able to own them but what *kinds* of weapons people should be able to own and under what *conditions* they can carry them.

Laying Down Your Life for Others

Still, a few Christian denominations, such as the Brethren and Mennonites, believe that all violence or killing is wrong for believers. They are opposed to Christ's followers *ever* taking the life of another human being. While violence clearly existed in Old Testament times, *pacifists* such as these believe we should look to Jesus having willingly laid down his life for us as our example. Even more, Jesus calls his followers to "take up [their] cross" and do the same for others (Mark 8:34).

Some are quick to label pacifism as weak or cowardly, but this is a gross misunderstanding. Pacifist reformers like Martin Luther King Jr. model how nonviolent resistance can lead to moral revolution. While I am not a pacifist, I have deep admiration for Christians who are willing to lay down their lives in trusting God before using violence against other human beings (see 1 Peter 2:21-23).

The Case for Guns

In contrast to pacifism, many Christians believe they have a right to self-defense, including owning a gun, *because* they are pro-life. Author Karen Swallow Prior jogs thirty-five to forty miles per week. Given that she is a woman and sometimes runs alone, she feels the need to be vigilant about self-defense. One male driver pulled up next to her and asked if she wanted a ride. Another man exposed himself to her as she jogged by. As a result of these kinds of experiences, her husband bought her a small gun to carry when she jogs. How does she justify this as a Christian? She explains, "While as a Christian I try to cultivate my willingness to lay down my life for the sake of the gospel or for the life of another, I don't believe I'm supposed to risk my life for a would-be rapist. To me, being pro-life means protecting my own life too."[3]

The best defense for the moral right to own a gun is grounded in the right to life, as we see in Karen's example. If a gun is necessary for self-defense, then owning a gun can be justified as a means of securing the right to life. Although a good case can be made that people need guns for hunting and can enjoy them recreationally (as in skeet shooting), defending oneself and others is the strongest argument for the right to own and use a gun.

The Bible and Guns

While the Bible obviously doesn't mention guns, it does seem to allow for acting in self-defense. For example, if an Israelite killed a thief who was breaking into their home at night, they were not guilty of a crime (see Exodus 22:2). And Nehemiah encouraged the city wall's builders to carry weapons to fend off intruders (see Nehemiah 4:1-23).

Perhaps the most common verse used to indicate that Christians can defend themselves is Jesus telling his disciples before his arrest to buy a sword (see Luke 22:36). Detective J. Warner Wallace asks, "Why would Jesus say this? At the very least, Jesus was calling His disciples to prepare themselves for their own defense. And the sword (a killing instrument) was evidently permissible in the eyes of Jesus."[4]

Wallace may be right here, but we also need to keep in mind that just a few verses later, Jesus scolded one of his disciples who used a sword to cut off the ear of the high priest's slave. Jesus said, "No more of this!" and then healed the slave's ear (Luke 22:49-51). Many scholars take this passage as Jesus rebuking his disciples for taking him literally.

Others who defend the right to use weapons in self-defense point to the fact that the New Testament does not condemn soldiers for being in the military. When John the Baptist was preaching a message of repentance, some soldiers asked him how they should respond, and he said, "Do not extort money from anyone by threats or by false accusation, and be content with your wages" (Luke 3:14). If laying down your sword is always the right thing to do, then why didn't John mention this? In another case, instead of rebuking a Roman centurion's occupation, Jesus commends the man as a model of faith (see Matthew 8:5-13). If the use of force is forbidden for a follower of Jesus, shouldn't we expect some indication that soldiers seeking to honor God should leave their profession or lay down their arms?

While this case is certainly not airtight, the Bible does seem to allow for the use of force in some instances.

Three Bad Arguments about Guns and Violence

Before we close this chapter, let's briefly consider three bad arguments about guns and violence.

"Violence Never Fixes Anything"

While sometimes violence encourages more violence, it is false to claim that violence never fixes anything. Violence helped end the Holocaust. Violence helped free slaves in the Civil War. Violence doesn't fix everything, but it can help to fix some things.

"Guns Don't Kill People; People Do"

This is a false dilemma. It is not either guns *or* people, but people *using* guns. While it is true that people can kill with other kinds of weapons, guns can more easily be used to carry out mass killings. The fact that people are the ultimate cause of gun violence is not a good argument against reasonable restrictions on gun ownership.

"No Law Can Prevent All Gun Violence"

This is true, but why should we resist laws that help reduce *some* violence, even if we can't stop *all* violence? The question should not be whether a policy stops all gun violence but whether it genuinely helps reduce gun violence without eliminating the right to own a gun.

What Can We Do?

Consider three steps Christians can take:

1. *If you own a gun, be careful to avoid idolatry.* The Bible
   cautions against trusting weapons and violence. Psalm
   44:6-7 says, "For not in my bow do I trust, nor can my
   sword save me. But you [God] have saved us from our
   foes." If you need a gun to believe you are in control
   or to make you feel secure, then your gun may have
   become an idol.

2. *We should avoid naive laws or mandates that overlook
   humanity's capacity for evil.* Some laws mandate gun-
   free zones with the good intention that it will stop
   or reduce gun violence. However, shooters may be
   more willing to enter such zones since they have no
   fear of someone armed trying to stop them. My point
   is not about the effectiveness of gun-free zones but
   that we need genuinely effective laws, not just good
   intentions.

3. *We should pursue effective laws that will actually help
   to restrain humanity's capacity for evil.* The Bible
   teaches that the human heart is desperately sinful (see
   Jeremiah 17:9; Mark 7:14-23; Romans 3:9-18). All
   human beings (including those who use guns) have
   a deeply fallen nature and are capable of great evil.
   Thus, shouldn't we work for reasonable gun laws to

minimize harm to others? We can debate those laws, but it seems that every Christian should be committed to supporting laws that minimize the effects of human sinfulness and protect human lives.

23

Immigration

⚡

On a warm May night, at least seventy-four people, including women and children, squeezed into a trailer headed to Houston, Texas. They were eagerly anticipating a new life. Many were excited to meet up with their friends and family who had come to America earlier. Tragically, the truck became so sweltering hot that nineteen of the passengers died of suffocation, hyperthermia, and dehydration.[1]

Raul Gomez-Garcia is an illegal immigrant who is presently serving an eighty-year prison sentence for ambushing two cops. Though he was a gang member in Los Angeles, Gomez-Garcia fled to Mexico after the shooting, where he was later caught and sent back to the United States for sentencing. Of the two police officers Gomez-Garcia shot, one of them, Donald Young, died on the spot. Young left behind his widow and two daughters, who were understandably devastated.[2]

At sixteen years old, José Antonio Gutiérrez came to Los Angeles without legal papers from Guatemala. Orphaned as a child, he joined the Marines to help pay for his university education. He was grateful to the United States for giving him a chance. He was one of the first casualties of the Iraq war and was granted citizenship a month after his death.[3]

Immigration Is Complicated

Each of these stories is a tragedy. It is a tragedy that some people have lost their lives fleeing to the United States (thousands have died this way). It is a tragedy that some American citizens have been the victims of car wrecks, robberies, and other crimes at the hands of undocumented immigrants. It is a tragedy that a young man like José, who left his home country looking for a better life, was unable to realize his dreams of citizenship, education, and a prosperous life in the United Staets.

Immigration is a complicated issue. It is an emotional one too. Think about it. On the one hand, if you were living in another country that limited your ability to be free and possibly even put you and your loved ones at risk, wouldn't you want to come to this country? No question about it. The United States is an unparalleled nation that offers freedom, security, and opportunity. On the other hand, if you were an American citizen and you or your loved ones were threatened or harmed by an undocumented immigrant, wouldn't you want stronger borders and more enforcement? Again, of course you would.

There are legitimate questions and concerns on all sides of this issue. The goal of this chapter is not to find simple answers. There aren't any. The goal is to bring balance to a complicated issue. We aim to find a balance between overly strict border enforcement and indiscriminate borders that are open to anyone who wants to enter.

Above all, as followers of Jesus, we need to think Christianly about immigration. With that in mind, our goal is not just to get the issue right but to learn how to love our fellow citizens and immigrants better. Isn't that what Jesus would do?

Defining our Terms

Let's begin by defining a few terms. There is an important difference between a refugee and an immigrant. A *refugee* is someone who has fled their home country because of safety concerns. Many Syrian refugees have left their home country in fear for their lives and have settled in various countries throughout Europe and beyond. Some refugees have also fled various countries in South America, seeking asylum in the United States and Canada.

In contrast, *immigrants* choose to leave their homeland

for another country where they can become permanent residents or citizens. Many are children. Some immigrants enter their new countries legally, and others enter illegally.

It is important to keep in mind that people immigrate for a range of different reasons. Some flee their home country for survival, some are looking for a better life, and some immigrate for less noble reasons. Understanding why people have immigrated can help us understand how best to relate to them.

Christians and Immigration

As with many other issues we have approached in this book, the place to begin is the recognition that immigrants are made in the image of God. This seems obvious, but often immigration debates focus solely on economic impact, national security, or cultural identity. These are important issues, yet as Christians, we must begin the conversation with a recognition of the *humanity* of immigrants rather than the best policy regarding immigrants. We must approach the conversation with a caring demeanor and a desire to love immigrants.

Most immigrants are motivated to find a better life for their families, yet many struggle to adapt to their new homes. Can you imagine how tough it would be to learn a new language, eat new food, and live in an entirely new country? Immigrating to a new country is often motivated by the desire to make a better life for a family, but that doesn't mean it's an easy life. The more we recognize that, the better we're positioned to think about loving our immigrant neighbors.

And yet, people living in a host country are also made in the image of God. *Their* needs are important too. As Markus Zehnder has noted, "Love can also be expected on the side of the migrants. It is not an act of love when illegal immigrants . . . benefit from a foreign country's welfare system. It is also not an act of love when illegal immigrants put migrants who abide by laws in a position of relative disadvantage. . . . It is not an act of love when immigrants do not respect the hosts."[4] Christians must find a way to show love and support to both immigrants *and* citizens of the host country.

The Bible and Immigration

While there are considerable differences between biblical times and today, the Bible has a lot to say about how we should treat immigrants. Let's consider two big points.

Point #1: God Cares for Immigrants

The Bible begins with a command for people to spread across the earth ("Multiply and fill the earth"—Genesis 1:28). Consider how many key figures in the Bible were either immigrants or refugees:

- *Abraham* left his home country and sought refuge in Egypt on his way to the Promised Land.

- *Joseph* was forcibly taken to Egypt, and later his family joined him during a famine.
- *Moses* fled from Pharaoh to the land of Midian.
- *Ruth* became an immigrant in Bethlehem.
- *Daniel* was carried off to Babylon.
- *Joseph* and *Mary* fled to Egypt with *Jesus* during Herod's slaughter of the children of Bethlehem. They later moved to Nazareth.

Can you see how central movement is to the Bible? Whether for safety or because of a call from God, immigrants and refugees appear throughout the Bible. It is interesting to note that these immigrants are not a problem for God's plan, but instead, God works through them to further carry out his plan!

And yet, Markus Zehnder offers an important qualifier: "The biblical flight stories cannot be used to support the argument for liberal immigration policies, because they have no direct connection with the current phenomenon of mass-(im)migration."[5] In other words, while God clearly has a heart for immigrants—and he has worked immigration into his divine plan—it does not follow that Christians must support certain statewide immigration policies. These are different issues.

Point #2: God Commands His Followers to Care for Immigrants

God not only cares about immigrants; he commands his followers to care for them too.

IMMIGRATION IN THE OLD TESTAMENT

There are a few Hebrew words often translated as "foreigner," "resident alien," "stranger," and "immigrant" in English Bibles. While there are many political, cultural, and theological differences between Old Testament times and our own, Scripture consistently demonstrates God's heart for outsiders. The Israelites were not to mistreat the foreigners in their midst because they had been foreigners in Egypt for four hundred years (see Exodus 22:21). The people of Israel were commanded not to strip their vineyards bare so sojourners and the poor could glean them for food (see Leviticus 19:10). Immigrants were to receive part of the tithes so they could eat (see Deuteronomy 26:12). And there were serious consequences for Israelites who took advantage of immigrants (see Deuteronomy 27:19).

Because of the historic differences between ancient Israel and today, as well as the focus these passages place on a limited number of individuals, these biblical commands should not be transferred to state laws involving mass immigration. But they do show God's desire that Christians treat outsiders, such as immigrants, with care and concern.

JESUS AND IMMIGRATION

While Jesus never spoke directly about immigration, he and his family were refugees in Egypt when Herod wanted to kill him. He also pushed the boundaries of who his followers were supposed to love, as we see in the story of the Good Samaritan. In response to the question, "Who is my neighbor?" Jesus included the Samaritans, who were despised foreigners to the Jews (see Luke 10:25-37). Would Jesus include immigrants among those we are supposed to love? Of course!

And yet, this is not a story about mass migration. The Good Samaritan made a free choice on a personal level and used his own time and resources to help a neighbor in need. This story is not about whether Samaritans should be accepted as immigrants.

Jesus clearly taught that we should love our neighbors, including immigrants. Our love for others should have no ethnic or social boundaries. Yet Jesus did not address the political issue of mass migration. We must be careful not to confuse his command to love our neighbors with certain policy issues. These are different matters.

Should Christians Follow the Law?

Am I suggesting we dismiss the law? No! God ordained governments to protect and care for their own citizens. Like a mother who cares for her kids, governments have an obligation to care for their citizens. Unauthorized immigration does raise legitimate national security concerns. Any nation is unwise to have lax immigration policies that allow *anyone* through its borders without knowing who they are and where they came from.

The apostle Paul says to "be subject to the governing authorities," which exist "for your good" (Romans 13:1, 4).

The apostle Peter says, "Be subject for the Lord's sake to every human institution" (1 Peter 2:13). Clearly, Christians are called to respect governing authorities. How do we balance the commands to love outsiders *and* respect governing authorities? Professor Daniel Carroll helps:

> If one begins with a biblical orientation that includes the centrality of the importance of the immigrant as made in the image of God, if one can appreciate how pervasive migration experiences are to the history and faith of the people of God, if Old Testament law projects an ethics of compassion, and if the thrust of Jesus' ministry and the New Testament as a whole is to love the outsider and be hospitable, then the inclination is to be charitable to the immigrant in the name of God and Christ.[6]

In other words, Christians need to find the balance between supporting just immigration laws *and* loving immigrants in our midst. Like most issues in this book, the challenge is to be both loving and just.

While this issue is complicated, Scott Rae offers a few reasonable goals that should guide immigration policy for countries:

1. Control borders and set limits on immigration.
2. Meet the immediate needs of desperate refugees
3. Ensure that immigrants are not dangerous to the community.

4. Ensure that public services don't limit resources for citizens.

5. Offer a fair process of citizenship for all who seek to enter the country.

6. Keep immediate families together whenever possible.[7]

What Christians Can Do

To end this chapter, I simply want to give you one personal challenge: *find a way to love an immigrant.* Is there someone at your school, in your community, or on a sports team that you can befriend? Listen to them. Hear their stories. Ask about their family. Be curious about their life and what it's like for them in the United States. Learn from them. Try to treat them as you would want them to treat you if you were an immigrant. Isn't that what Jesus would do?

24
Artificial Intelligence
⚡

A FEW YEARS AGO, one of my former high school students, Emilee, enrolled in a large state university in the Midwest. On the first day of English class, the professor told the students that within the next few decades, robots were likely going to overtake human beings in their intelligence and capabilities. He expressed hope (and concern) that these robots would care for their lesser evolved human neighbors: *us*.

Curious as to how this might happen, Emilee posed a thoughtful question for the professor: "How can a physical object such as a robot ever become self-conscious?" Without missing a beat, the professor shot back, "Do you actually believe in the reality of the soul?" When she said yes, the entire class laughed at her.

Emilee experienced a clash of worldviews. Her professor and many of her fellow students were *naturalists* and thus believed that human beings had emerged through an unguided, purposeless evolutionary process. In this view, humans are basically complex biological machines. If so, it would seem possible that robots *could* come to think someday. If we live in a naturalistic universe and humans are the highest form of evolution, then why can't scientists build robots that mimic the human brain? Within this worldview, that seems reasonable.

But what if the professor is wrong about the nature of reality? What if we live in a *supernatural* universe and things like God, angels, and heaven are real? What if a human being is both body and soul, as the Bible teaches?[1] If so, then robots will continue to develop the capacity to perform remarkable functions, but they will *never* be able to think. They can execute processes that mimic human thinking, but they will never be conscious. In fact, if thinking requires a soul, then trying to build a conscious robot is as fruitless as trying to turn lead into gold. Given the nature of reality, it *can't* happen.

Science Fiction and Artificial Intelligence

When I mention artificial intelligence (AI) to my students, they typically think of movies like *The Terminator* or *I, Robot*, in which robots somehow develop consciousness and enslave humanity. But this is only one small part of the equation. Even if robots don't take over the world—not holding my breath!—AI affects our lives *right now* and is increasingly shaping the world around us.

AI systems enable self-driving cars, are used by businesses to sort through job applicants, help diagnose sicknesses and perform surgeries, are used in warfare, and execute a range of other tasks. Consider a few that likely influence you right now:

- Amazon uses sophisticated algorithms to track every product you (and millions of other people) visit or buy and causes similar products to appear on your screen in hopes you will buy them.

- Netflix gathers data from you every time you watch a show and offers recommendations based upon your viewing habits. The algorithms include what you watch, when you watch it, how long you watch it, and many other factors that help the system grow "smarter" over time. Netflix even has an algorithm that offers tailor-made images to subscribers to get them to binge-watch as long as possible.[2]

- Social media platforms use algorithms to track your online behavior (videos you watch, images you like, posts you make) and manipulate their systems to keep you engaged as long as possible.

- Uber is able to operate because of an AI-based program that connects drivers and riders. The algorithm manages the number of drivers on the road at certain times. Uber couldn't afford to employ the thousands of people that would otherwise be necessary for these tasks, which the algorithm does instantaneously.[3]

It is tempting to think that we autonomously choose which products to buy, social media platforms to engage, or movies to watch. But did you know that 80 percent of TV shows and movies people watch on Netflix are discovered through the recommendation system?[4] When you sit down to watch a show on Netflix, your choices are undoubtedly influenced by an algorithm that has configured a pool of options tailored to your tastes.

Are these AI systems bad? Not necessarily. When looking for an action movie, I don't want to wade through a bunch of romance films (unless my wife is with me, of course). You may have different tastes, but you probably appreciate Amazon suggesting products that interest you. Technology can be good, but we also have to be wise and discerning about how companies attempt to manipulate us.

And some artificial intelligence systems are much more nefarious. Consider social media bots,[5] programs designed to do various tasks *as if they were human*. While they can be used to encourage civic engagement (such as voting), they can also be programmed to spread hate speech, manipulate elections, and attempt to sway public opinion. Because they appear human, these kinds of AI programs require much more of our wisdom to identity.

Avoiding Two Big Temptations

With the increasing technology of AI, there are two temptations we must avoid.

The Temptation to Act Like God

While my kids grew up watching Marvel and DC superhero movies, I grew up watching the original Star Wars films. One of the scenes that captured my imagination was when Luke Skywalker got a robotic hand to replace the real one Darth Vader cut off in battle. While this technology was science fiction in the early 1980s, now AI is being used to allow amputees or people born with disabilities to control prosthetic limbs through their thoughts. That's right: their *thoughts*. Some of these prosthetic limbs are even stronger and more resilient than flesh-and-blood limbs.

This is truly astonishing technology that will improve the lives of countless people. But it also raises some thorny questions: Is there a difference between fixing a problem (such as a lost limb) and enhancing our bodies beyond their natural limits? How far can we take this? Will such technology turn people into "machines" that can be manipulated for some benefit? Will it favor the rich who can afford such enhancements and create more of a disparity between the haves and the have-nots?

This same kind of temptation has existed since the dawn of civilization. Even though their technology was considerably less modern—brick and stone—people built the Tower of Babel to reach the heavens and make a name for themselves (see Genesis 11:1-9). They used their existing technology to be gods over the world around them.

Part of the drive to develop AI technology is to help counter the effects of the Fall. Helping people who are hurting is good! But much is also driven by the desire for power, fame, and control. We are afraid of suffering. We are afraid of losing control. We are afraid of death. So we use technology to fight against our fears and delay the inevitable. We use technology to be gods ourselves.

Technology can be wonderful. But we must learn from the people at the Tower of Babel and resist the temptation to use it as a substitute for trusting God.

The Temptation to Replace Relationships

The futurist movie *Her* is about a middle-aged man, Theodore, who "dates" an operating system named Samantha. Theodore is intrigued by her ability to grow and learn, and they bond over discussions about life and relationships.

What would motivate someone to "date" an artificially intelligent computer program? The movie is science *fiction*, of course. But to make it believable, Theodore is depressed and lonely because of a pending divorce from his high school sweetheart. The movie works for two reasons. First, we see his desperation for connection, even if that means settling for something artificial. And second, we each face the temptation today to avoid the hard work of real relationships and to settle for a counterfeit.

How so? Many people settle for the false intimacy of porn rather than doing the hard work of building real relationships. Many build false social media images to cover up the hurt in their lives. Many people get lost in their social media feed rather than connecting with those physically around them.

Technology can be a great way to foster healthy relationships, but it can never *replace* them. A digital "like" cannot replace a physical hug. Staring at a screen cannot replace staring into another person's eyes. Meaningful relationships require honesty, commitment, and presence. We must not allow the lure of technology to replace the deep yearning of our hearts. Only relationships with God and other people can do that.

What Christians Can Do

Here are two important steps for how Christians can respond to our increasingly digital world:

1. *Build flesh-and-blood relationships.* Technology is a wonderful tool, but it cannot replace face-to-face relationships. Don't let technology hinder or replace real relationships with family, friends, and neighbors.

2. *Always filter new technology through a Christian world-view.* When you see a new form of AI, ask yourself a few questions: Will this enhance human relationships or harm them? Does this dignify people as image bearers of God? Will this technology tempt people to "play God"?

PART 6

Cultural
Engagement

25

Knowing God's Will

⚡

ONE OF THE MOST COMMON QUESTIONS I receive from young Christians is "How can I know the will of God for my life?" To be honest, this question deeply troubled me for many years. What does God want from me? What if I miss God's will? For several difficult years, I viewed God's will as something hidden—like an encoded message on a treasure map. I thought my job was to search around while God sent little hints, saying, "You're getting warmer!" Other times, I feared that God's will would only be revealed to me if he took something I loved—such as basketball—away from me. While other people seemed to have confidence about knowing God's will, I felt no such assurance.

Knowing God's will is no longer a problem for me, and it should not be for you, either. There are a few biblical principles I have learned about the will of God that have transformed how I make decisions. In the next few pages, I would like to share them with you.

The Bible and God's Will

Keep in mind that much of God's will has already been revealed in Scripture.

If you read all the passages in the Bible that mention "the will of God" or "God's will," you will discover that they fall into two broad categories. First, God has a *moral* will for us, which involves living the way he has designed us to live. This involves avoiding sexual immorality, honoring our parents, and being conformed to the character of Christ (as we will see below).

Second, God has a *sovereign* will, which stems from his total control of the universe. Ephesians 1:11 says that God "works all things according to the counsel of his will." Daniel 4:35 says that God "does according to his will." God is sovereignly moving history toward his desired ends. Unless God reveals it to us, we don't know God's sovereign will. But God *has* revealed his moral will.

Let's consider five truths about God's moral will for your life:

1. *God's will is that you be saved.* The first aspect of God's will is that people be saved by believing in God's Son,

Jesus Christ. Paul says in 1 Timothy 2:4 that God "desires all people to be saved and to come to the knowledge of the truth." It is God's will that people turn to him in repentance and be saved. If you are stumbling through life trying to know God's will but have never asked God to forgive your sins, then you are not even in the beginning of God's will. Qualification number one for God's will is your salvation.

2. *God's will is that you be filled with the Holy Spirit.* At the moment of salvation, the Holy Spirit enters the life of every Christian. As a result, you have the potential to live a bold life of faith if you are willing to surrender control of your life to him. One task of the Holy Spirit is to convict us of sin and lead us to develop certain "fruits of the Spirit" such as gentleness, patience, love, and self-control (see Galatians 5:16-24). It is always amazing to me how few Christians realize this powerful truth. When I hear Christians say, "God, send me your Spirit," I often wonder why they don't realize that God is already present in their lives (see 1 Corinthians 6:19)! The Holy Spirit is not a force that comes in doses; he is a person who lives within you, and God wants us to live by his strength.

3. *God's will is that you be pure.* When young Christians ask me about God's will, I often take them directly to 1 Thessalonians 4:3: "For this is the will of God, your sanctification: that you abstain from sexual

immorality." It doesn't get much clearer than this! God's desire for every Christian is that he or she be sexually pure and grow in sanctification (which means becoming more like Christ). It is absurd for a young Christian who is disobeying God's plan for sex to say, "God, reveal your will to me." Since that person is ignoring God's moral will, why should God reveal some further will?

4. *God's will is that you submit to proper authorities.* First Peter 2:18 says, "Be submissive to your masters [which for you can be your parents, teachers, coaches] with all respect. . . ." You might be thinking, *But, Sean, you don't know my parents.* But the verse continues, "not only to those who are good and gentle, but also to those who are *unreasonable*" (NASB1995). How should you respond to unreasonable parents? Submit.

   Is there ever a time to disobey authorities? Sure. The midwives disobeyed the Egyptian authorities that commanded them to kill newborn Hebrew babies (see Exodus 1), and God protected them. The time to disobey authorities is when they ask you to do something that violates God's higher law—not when they are being unreasonable.

5. *God's will is that you trust him when you suffer.* Being a Christian is not always easy. You may be *persecuted* for following Jesus. Anyone who tries to tell you differently is watering down the message of Christ. This

is why the apostle Peter wrote, "It is better to suffer for doing good, if that should be God's will, than for doing evil" (1 Peter 3:17). You might get left out for not partying. You might get called a bigot for embracing the biblical view of sex and gender. And you may be mocked for sharing your faith. God's will is that you trust him nonetheless.

The takeaway here is that much of God's will has been revealed in Scripture. Trust God to work out his sovereign will as you obey his moral will. Sadly, many people live their lives ignoring God's moral will, trying to uncover his hidden will, while never actually trusting his sovereign will. What a tragedy!

Seek Wisdom above Gold and Silver

What about God's individual will for your life? Here's the surprising truth: the Bible does not teach that God has a hidden will for your life that you need to uncover before making decisions.

Then how do you choose a college, career, or spouse? The answer is found in seeking wisdom. Proverbs 16:16 says, "How much better to get wisdom than gold! To get understanding is to be chosen rather than silver." God does not make choices for us. He has given us the freedom to decide.

Then how can you become wise?

First, *humble yourself before God.* God is the Creator; you are the creature. God is infinite; you are finite. God knows everything; you don't. Proverbs 9:10 says, "Fear of the LORD is the beginning of wisdom." Wisdom begins by recognizing our proper relationship before God and obeying everything he has revealed in the Bible. Part of humbling ourselves involves obedience to God's moral will. There is no wisdom in disobedience.

Second, *ask God for wisdom*. James 1:5 says, "If any of you lacks wisdom, let him ask God, who gives generously to all without reproach, and it will be given him." Pray that God will make you wise, and the Bible promises that he will.

Third, *seek counsel from others*. Proverbs 15:22 says, "Without counsel plans fail, but with many advisers they succeed." One of the best ways to get wisdom is to ask trusted leaders in your life—parents, coaches, teachers, pastors, and so on—for advice and direction.

Does this guarantee you will always make good decisions? No. I have made many poor decisions in my life, but I have learned from them and moved on. God may not always prevent us from making bad decisions, but he does promise to be with us every step of the way and to conform our character to be more like Jesus. Proverbs 16:9 says, "The heart of man plans his way, but the LORD establishes his steps."

God's Will Is *You*

Remember, God's will is that you be saved, be filled with the Holy Spirit, be sexually pure, submit to the proper authorities, trust God when you suffer, and develop wisdom. The Bible makes it very clear that this is God's will for your life. Yet you might still be thinking, *What about God's* specific *will for my life? I thought you were going to tell me where I should go to college or how to find my spouse!*

Here's the final lesson of this chapter. God's will is not something hidden that you have to find. Rather, God's will is *you*. You see, God is more concerned with the type of person you are becoming and how that shapes the way you love him and others than he is about where you go to college or the kind of student you become. God is less concerned with where you live than with how you treat your neighbors. God is less concerned with who you take to prom than with the way you treat your date. God's will is that you are conformed to the image of his Son.

God's will is *you*.

26

A Guide for Conversations

⚡

HAVE YOU EVER HAD A CONVERSATION go badly? Of course. We all have. If you reflect for a moment, I bet you can think of a painful conversation that did not go as you intended. To be honest, I can think of a lot (and many were my fault)!

When conversations go poorly, there can be a temptation to avoid them in the future. After all, who wants to get into an argument? Aren't we told to avoid discussing politics and religion? We have considered some deeply controversial issues in this book. Given the sensitive nature of issues such as race, gender, and gun control, is it really worth entering into conversations about them, especially if you might get labeled a bigot or a hater?

Here's my answer: *we must be willing to have these difficult conversations with Christians and non-Christians alike.* Being disengaged is not an option for followers of Jesus. It may make us rebels, but we must be willing to speak truth uncompromisingly and to do so with kindness. This book has given you many examples of Christians who live and speak biblical truth and who are motivated by love and compassion. That's what we need today more than ever! Will that be you?

Remember the Main Goal

You might recall the example I shared in chapter 3 about my "atheist encounter" presentations, in which I role-play an atheist to Christian audiences. Sadly, there are often some critical and harsh responses aimed at my atheist character.

One reason for this is that many Christians have not thought about why they believe as they do. Many lack depth in their convictions, so when I press them, they naturally get defensive. One goal of this book is to give you the confidence to have conversations with people who see the world differently. If you have stayed with me this far, then you have enough knowledge to engage in meaningful conversations. Don't get overconfident, as there is much more to learn, but don't underestimate yourself either.

A second reason some Christians get defensive at my atheist role-play is that they don't have a loving heart toward others. They are more interested in sounding smart or proving a point than in truly loving other people. I hope that is not you. Above all, Scripture calls us to love God and love other people. That's why we're here!

Does it do any good to win an argument if you did not treat the other person with love? No! Paul says that if you have prophetic powers or faith that moves mountains but don't have love, then you are nothing. If you give away all you have, including your own life, but don't have love, then you gain nothing for your sacrifice (see 1 Corinthians 13:1-3).

Remember, the goal of a conversation is not to sound smart. It's not to be right. The point is to love someone. Love certainly requires speaking the truth, in the right time and the right manner, but our greatest goal in engaging others must always be to love them. Period.

A Simple Guide for Meaningful Conversations

Hopefully right now you're thinking, *Okay, I want to have conversations with people about issues that matter. But where do I start?* In my experience, I have found that most people are willing to have civil conversations with others if we ask good questions and treat them respectfully.

Here are four practical questions I regularly use in my conversations.[1] You can apply this approach to all the issues in this book and more. I often use this approach in spiritual conversations with skeptics as well.

Question #1: What Do You Believe?

A great place to begin a conversation is finding out what the other person actually believes. How is this done? Simple: *listen.* Proverbs 18:13 says, "If one gives an answer before he hears, it is his folly and shame."

Have you ever felt like someone wanted to tell you what they believe but was not interested in hearing what you believe? That doesn't feel good, does it? Good listening is a way of loving people. Poor listening is a way of dismissing them.

If you want to love someone, listen to them. Ask clarifying questions. Don't cut them off. Give eye contact. Turn off your phone. This shows people you care about them and what they believe.

Question #2: Why Do You Believe It?

Once we understand *what* the other person believes, the next step is to find out *why* they believe it. The best way to find out is to ask! Since guesses are often wrong, why not say, "Thanks for sharing your views on [immigration, race, gender, etc.]. Can you share with me why you hold that view?" Then listen and try to understand.

Proverbs 20:5 says, "The purpose in a man's heart is like deep water, but a man of understanding will draw it out." People have deep reasons for their beliefs. Some are intellectual, but many are emotional, relational, or experiential. A teen immigrant recently shared her views on immigration with me and how they were deeply shaped by her life experience. Can you see how her experience would deeply inform her views on immigration? The same can be true with someone's views on race, gun control, and any other issue.

Question #3: Where Do We Agree?

One of the best ways to have a meaningful conversation with someone is to find areas of agreement. Proverbs 24:3 says, "By wisdom a house is built, and by understanding it is established." Common ground helps break down walls between people and fosters understanding.

A few years ago, I visited an atheist group and sat on the hot seat for a couple of hours while they asked me dozens of questions. Even though we have radically different worldviews, the host expressed how amazed he was that we had so much in common. In conversations, I often look to find where the person's worldview overlaps with the Christian worldview. Rather than focusing initially on where we disagree, I begin by looking for common ground.

Question #4: Where Do We Disagree and Why?

After I understand what someone believes and why they believe it, and once I have found common ground, I often shift the conversation to focus on where we disagree and why. I have found it helpful to get to the heart of an issue and clarify the reason for our disagreement.

For instance, consider the issue of poverty. Most people

agree that we should help the poor. But they differ over the best way to help them. Both Marxists and Christians want to help the poor, but their approaches differ radically. Why? The answer lies in their views of human nature. Marxists think humans are naturally good and that greed comes from inequity in society. But Jesus said greed comes from the human heart. Christians and Marxists have a similar desire to alleviate the suffering of the poor but differ radically about policy because of their clashing views of human nature.

Finding out where you differ from someone and why can lead to a productive conversation. It can also lead to ways that you can work together with people for the common good. This doesn't mean we can find common cause on every issue. Even though I have treated him graciously, a prominent atheist publicly called me a bigot for not embracing same-sex marriage. I try to find common cause with people from different backgrounds, but when all is said and done, I cannot compromise the biblical view on marriage. To do so would be to be unfaithful to Scripture and unloving to my neighbor.

Final Challenge

I am honored you have stayed with me to the end of this book. Kudos for caring about having a deep faith *and* about learning how to engage those around you in thoughtful conversations.

Here is my final challenge: *speak the truth in love*. Don't buy the lie that love involves softening truth or the other lie that callously and foolishly says the truth is only and always loving. Jesus said it is *truth* that sets us free. And yet we must not speak truth without genuine concern for and understanding of others. It's not truth *or* love—it's truth *and* love. When you live this way, it may make you a rebel. But even Jesus was considered a rebel in his day.

If you follow this example of Jesus, I am confident God can use you to make a genuine difference in the lives of other people.

Go for it!

Let's connect! If you have stayed with me to the end of this book, consider finding me online. I use a variety of different social media platforms, but in particular, check out YouTube. I have regular conversations with people from a variety of backgrounds on the very topics covered in this book. I do many livestreams and would love to see you there!

Acknowledgments

⚡

MY THANKS TO A NUMBER OF people who made this book possible. As always, Mark Sweeney did a fantastic job connecting me with the right publisher. And thanks to Jon Farrar and the team at Tyndale for believing in this book. Thanks to both Dana Dill and Jonathan Schindler for excellent edits. And I want to express my personal gratitude to all the Christians who stand boldly for their faith, as rebels today and in the past, and follow the example of Jesus.

Notes

⚡

CHAPTER 1: STANDING FOR WHAT IS RIGHT

1. See Peter Kreeft, *Making Choices: Practical Wisdom for Everyday Moral Decisions* (Ann Arbor, MI: Servant, 1990), 1–2.
2. John Stonestreet, "BreakPoint: The U.S. Women's Soccer Team and Jaelene Hinkle," BreakPoint, June 27, 2019, https://www.breakpoint.org/breakpoint-the-u-s-womens-soccer-team-and-jaelene-hinkle/.

CHAPTER 2: BECOMING A GOOD PERSON

1. From David Kinnaman, president of the Barna Research Group, at a meeting at Barna on May 21, 2019.

CHAPTER 6: SMARTPHONES AND SOCIAL MEDIA

1. "Motor Vehicle Deaths Estimated to Have Dropped 2% in 2019," National Safety Council, February 20, 2020, https://www.nsc.org/newsroom/motor-vehicle-deaths-estimated-to-have-dropped-2-i.
2. Christina Gough, "Average Attendance at Division I FBS College Football Games from 2003 to 2019," Statista, September 20, 2021. https://bit.ly/3ab70nx.
3. Dr. Sean McDowell, "What Does the Bible say about Homosexuality? Sean McDowell and Matthew Vines in Conversation," YouTube video, February 3, 2018, https://www.youtube.com/watch?v=yFY4VtCWgyI.
4. Scott Slayton, "What Are the Marks of Genuine Friendship?," *One Degree to Another* (blog), Patheos, October 9, 2018, https://www.patheos.com/blogs/onedegreetoanother/2018/10/friendship/.

CHAPTER 8: POLITICS

1. "Dr. Martin Luther King's visit to Cornell College," Cornell College News Center, accessed August 14, 2020, https://news.cornellcollege .edu/dr-martin-luther-kings-visit-to-cornell-college/#:~:text=It%20 may%20be%20true%20that,do%20in%20society%20through%20 legislation.
2. Secularists think marriage is a union of two people who love each other (although some now question the necessity of *two*). Christians believe marriage is a permanent union specifically of one man and one woman that is oriented toward children.

CHAPTER 9: DRUGS AND ADDICTION

1. While long-standing research has shown that marijuana use harms memory, there is some evidence that at least some of the impairments reverse if the habit stops. See this recent study: Randi Melissa Schuster et al., "One Month of Cannabis Abstinence in Adolescents and Young Adults Is Associated with Improved Memory," *The Journal of Clinical Psychiatry* 79, no. 6 (October 30, 2018): 17m11977, https://www.psychiatrist.com /JCP/article/Pages/2018/v79/17m11977.aspx.
2. The YouTube channel C0nc0rdance is created by a cell biologist who is an atheist. He discusses the negative effects of marijuana and responds to charges that he cherry-picks research. See https://www.youtube.com /channel/UCPFnHiJx1P9UY05_F9sOu1g.
3. See "Marijuana: Just the Facts," *Drugs & Health Blog*, National Institute on Drug Abuse, May 6, 2019, https://teens.drugabuse.gov/blog/post /marijuana-just-facts.
4. John Stonestreet and Roberto Rivera, "Marijuana and Psychosis," BreakPoint, December 31, 2019, https://www.breakpoint.org/marijuana -and-psychosis/.
5. See "Tobacco, Nicotine, & Vaping (E-Cigarettes)," National Institute on Drug Abuse, June 25, 2021, https://teens.drugabuse.gov/drug-facts/tobacco -nicotine-vaping-e-cigarettes#topic-6.
6. Michael Joseph Blaha, "5 Vaping Facts You Need to Know," Johns Hopkins Medicine, accessed August 18, 2020, https://bit.ly/3g9vhvi.
7. The NIDA Blog Team, "The Latest on Vaping-Related Illness and Deaths," National Institute on Drug Abuse, April 6, 2020, https://teens .drugabuse.gov/blog/post/latest-vaping-related-illness-and-deaths.
8. "Is Vaping Better than Smoking?," American Heart Association, October 30, 2018, https://www.heart.org/en/healthy-living/healthy-lifestyle/quit-smoking -tobacco/is-vaping-safer-than-smoking.

CHAPTER 10: LONELINESS

1. Candice L. Odgers and Michael B. Robb, *Tweens, Teens, Tech, and Mental Health: Coming of Age in an Increasingly Digital, Uncertain, and Unequal World, 2020* (San Francisco, CA: Common Sense Media, 2020), 11, 17, https://www .commonsensemedia.org/research/tweens-teens-tech-and-mental-health.

CHAPTER 11: BULLYING

1. Jonathan McKee, *The Bullying Breakthrough: Real Help for Parents and Teachers of the Bullied, Bystanders, and Bullies* (Uhrichsville, OH: Shiloh Run Press, 2018), 17.
2. "Effects of Bullying," StopBullying.gov, U.S. Department of Health and Human Services, May 21, 2021, https://www.stopbullying.gov/bullying /effects.
3. "What Is Bullying," StopBullying.gov, U.S. Department of Health and Human Services, July 21, 2020, https://www.stopbullying.gov/bullying /what-is-bullying.
4. McKee, *The Bullying Breakthrough*, 11–12.
5. Neal Hardin, "What Does the Bible Teach Us about Bullying?" The Ethics & Religious Liberty Commission, September 26, 2018, https://erlc.com /resource-library/articles/what-does-the-bible-teach-us-about-bullying/.

CHAPTER 12: SUICIDE

1. Ryan Prior, "1 in 4 Young People Are Reporting Suicidal Thoughts. Here's How to Help," CNN, August 15, 2020, https://www.cnn.com/2020 /08/14/health/young-people-suicidal-ideation-wellness/index.html.
2. Sally C. Curtin and Melonie Heron, "Death Rates Due to Suicide and Homicide Among Persons Aged 10–24: United States, 2000–2017," *NCHS Data Brief*, No. 352 (Hyattsville, MD: National Center for Health Statistics, 2019), https://www.cdc.gov/nchs/data/databriefs/db352-h.pdf.
3. "Teen Suicide," Child Trends, accessed August 24, 2020, https://www .childtrends.org/indicators/suicidal-teens.
4. "Suicide Rising across the US: More Than a Mental Health Concern," Centers for Disease Control and Prevention, June 7, 2018, https://www .cdc.gov/vitalsigns/suicide/index.html.
5. Jonathan Noyes, "How to Make Sense of Suicide," Get a Grip 2020, https://www.livingoakschurch.org/getagrip (May 13, 2020).
6. Richard Dawkins, *River Out of Eden: A Darwinian View of Life* (New York: Basic Books, 1995), 133.
7. See Sean McDowell, "Could Judas Have Been Forgiven by Jesus?," June 2, 2020, https://seanmcdowell.org/blog/could-judas-have-repented.

CHAPTER 13: ASSISTED SUICIDE

1. Stephanie Gray Connors, *Start with What: 10 Principles for Thinking about Assisted Suicide* (Florida: Wongeese Publishing, 2021), 16.
2. See Wayne Grudem, *What the Bible Says about Abortion, Euthanasia, and End-of-life Medical Decisions* (Wheaton, IL: Crossway, 2020), 48–52.
3. Scott B. Rae, *Moral Choices: An Introduction to Ethics*, 4th ed. (Grand Rapids, MI: Zondervan, 2018), 256.
4. Peter Walker, "One in Five Dutch Doctors Would Help Physically Healthy Patients Die," *Guardian* (UK edition), February 17, 2015, https://bit.ly/35kPQDb.

CHAPTER 14: RACIAL TENSION

1. Thaddeus J. Williams, *Confronting Injustice without Compromising Truth: 12 Questions Christians Should Ask about Social Justice* (Grand Rapids, MI: Zondervan, 2020), 18.
2. The organization stands for values in opposition to the message of Jesus. Please see Sean McDowell, "Every Black Life Matters (But I Won't Support BLM)," June 11, 2020, https://seanmcdowell.org/blog/every-black-life-matters-but-i-wont-support-blm.
3. Thomas Sowell, *Intellectuals and Race* (New York: Basic Books, 2013), 4–5.
4. Dennis Prager, "5 Arguments Against 'America Is a Racist Country,'" *The Dennis Prager Show*, July 14, 2020, https://www.dennisprager.com/column/5-arguments-against-america-is-a-racist-country/.

CHAPTER 15: SEX

1. Rachel Gilson, *Born Again This Way: Coming Out, Coming to Faith, and What Comes Next* (Epsom, Surrey, England: The Good Book Company, 2020), 23.
2. Christopher West, *Theology of the Body for Beginners: Rediscovering the Meaning of Life, Love, Sex, and Gender*, rev. ed. (North Palm Beach, FL: Wellspring, 2018), 102.

CHAPTER 16: HOMOSEXUALITY

1. Rachel Gilson, *Born Again this Way: Coming Out, Coming to Faith, and What Comes Next*, (Epsom, Surrey, England: The Good Book Company, 2020), 25.
2. If you want to hear more of Rachel's story, check out my YouTube interview with her: "Christians and the LGBTQ Conversation: A Powerful Story of Redemption," August 27, 2020, https://www.youtube.com/watch?v=qbO-XtchZvc.

3. If you want more depth about God's design for sex, check out my student book *Chasing Love: Sex, Love, and Relationships in a Confused Culture* (Nashville, TN: B&H Publishing Group, 2020).

CHAPTER 17: TRANSGENDER IDEOLOGY

1. "J.K. Rowling Writes about Her Reasons for Speaking Out on Sex and Gender Issues," J. K. Rowling, June 10, 2020, https://www.jkrowling.com /opinions/j-k-rowling-writes-about-her-reasons-for-speaking-out-on-sex -and-gender-issues/.

2. Gordon Rayner, "Minister Orders Inquiry into 4,000 Percent Rise in Children Wanting to Change Sex," *Telegraph*, September 16, 2018, https:// www.telegraph.co.uk/politics/2018/09/16/minister-orders-inquiry-4000 -per-cent-rise-children-wanting/.

3. Anna Nobili et al., "Autistic Traits in Treatment-Seeking Transgender Adults," *Journal of Autism and Developmental Disorders* 48 (April 13, 2018): 3984–3994, https://doi.org/10.1007/s10803-018-3557-2.

4. Abigail Shrier, *Irreversible Damage: The Transgender Craze Seducing Our Daughters* (Washington, DC: Regnery Publishing, 2020), 3.

5. Shrier, *Irreversible Damage*, xxiv.

6. Check out this two-minute video of when I was invited on CNN to discuss transgenderism but was then rejected for being "too compassionate": https://www.youtube.com/watch?v=s1Rs2bu6f8E.

7. In California, parents can opt their kids out of sexual health education but not out of gender education. Starting in kindergarten, kids are taught to embrace transgender ideology. See Sean McDowell, "New California Health Standards Lack Diversity, Inclusion, and Openness," February 14, 2019, https://seanmcdowell.org/blog/new-california-health-standards-lack -diversity-inclusion-and-openness.

8. Consider watching a few YouTube videos of their stories: Corinna: https:// youtu.be/5pm-W0r-Xwo, Lady Boi: https://youtu.be/bd3TjUcredo, Rose of Dawn: https://youtu.be/hf_Ajljavy4, Kinesis: https://youtu.be /2QJMSw5HnWU, Jadis Argiope: https://youtu.be/vIxXD6a7xv0, and Kalvin Garrah: https://youtu.be/N5VCS0SOuMg.

9. Shrier, *Irreversible Damage*, 118.

10. Jiska Ristori and Thomas D. Steensma, "Gender Dysphoria in Childhood," *International Review of Psychiatry* 28, no. 1 (2016): 13–20, https://bit.ly /2E7quxE.

11. Paul Bracchi, "Mixed-Up Five-Year-Olds and the Alarming Growth of the Gender Identity Industry," *Daily Mail*, February 24, 2012, https://www

.dailymail.co.uk/news/article-2106215/Mixed-year-olds-alarming-growth
-gender-identity-industry.html.

12. Shrier, *Irreversible Damage*, 170.

CHAPTER 18: PORNOGRAPHY

1. "Porn in the Digital Age: New Research Reveals Ten Trends," Barna, April 6, 2016, https://www.barna.com/research/porn-in-the-digital-age-new-research -reveals-10-trends/.

2. Kate Conger, "Gag Order: Sex Workers Allege Mistreatment at Kink.com," *SF Weekly*, Feb 20, 2013, https://www.sfweekly.com/news/gag-order-sex -workers-allege-mistreatment-at-kink-com/.

3. "Porn Stars Speak Out," Collective Shout, accessed November 10, 2021, https://www.collectiveshout.org/porn_stars_speak_out.

4. Eric W. Owens et al., "The Impact of Internet Pornography on Adolescents: A Review of the Research," *Sexual Addiction and Compulsivity* 19, no. 1 (January 2012): 99–122, https://doi.org/10.1080/10720162.2012 .660431.

5. Grant Hilary Brenner, "4 Ways Porn Use Causes Problems," *Psychology Today*, March 5, 2018, https://www.psychologytoday.com/us/blog /experimentations/201803/4-ways-porn-use-causes-problems.

6. See Josh D. McDowell, *The Porn Epidemic: Facts, Stats, and Solutions*, Josh McDowell Ministry, updated January 20, 2019, https://s3.amazonaws .com/jmm.us/PDFs-Downloadable/The+Porn+Epidemic+-+Complete +Portfolio-1-20-19.pdf, 11.

7. For instance, the Colson Center has some short videos responding to claims like "Porn Is Victimless," https://whatwouldyousay.org/porn-is -victimless/. Or see my 2.5-minute YouTube video, "What's Wrong with Porn?," https://www.youtube.com/watch?v=oYL7vRQTSR4.

8. See fightthenewdrug.org.

CHAPTER 19: ABORTION

1. For a more in-depth look at this passage, see Greg Koukl, "What Exodus 21:22 Says about Abortion," Stand to Reason, February 4, 2013, https:// www.str.org/w/what-exodus-21-22-says-about-abortion.

2. Ronald Reagan, *Abortion and the Conscience of the Nation* (Sacramento: New Regency, 2000), 42.

3. Stephanie Gray, "Abortion: From Controversy to Civility," YouTube video, June 19, 2017, https://www.youtube.com/watch?v=DzzfSq2DEc4.

CHAPTER 20: THE ENVIRONMENT

1. Greta Thunberg, "'Our House Is on Fire': Greta Thunberg, 16, Urges Leaders to Act On Climate," *Guardian* (UK edition), January 25, 2019, https://www.theguardian.com/environment/2019/jan/25/our-house-is -on-fire-greta-thunberg16-urges-leaders-to-act-on-climate.

2. Emanuela Barbiroglio, "Generation Z Fears Climate Change More Than Anything Else," *Forbes*, December 9, 2019, https://www.forbes.com/sites /emanuelabarbiroglio/2019/12/09/generation-z-fears-climate-change -more-than-anything-else/#4832034c501b.

3. Alexandra D. Syphard et al., "Human Presence Diminishes the Importance of Climate in Driving Fire Activity across the United States," *Proceedings of the National Academy of Sciences* 114, no. 52 (December 11, 2017): 13750–55, https://doi.org/10.1073/pnas.1713885114.

4. Michael Shellenberger, *Apocalypse Never: Why Environmental Alarmism Hurts Us All* (New York: HarperCollins, 2020), 252.

5. Shellenberger, *Apocalypse Never*, 113.

6. Peter James Spielman, "UN Predicts Disaster if Global Warming Not Checked," Associated Press, June 29, 1989, https://apnews.com/article /bd45c372caf118ec99964ea547880cd0.

7. Ken Magnuson, *Invitation to Christian Ethics: Moral Reasoning and Contemporary Issues* (Grand Rapids, MI: Kregel, 2020), 449–451.

8. Shellenberger, *Apocalypse Never*, 264.

CHAPTER 21: POVERTY

1. Steve Corbett and Brian Fikkert, *When Helping Hurts: How to Alleviate Poverty without Hurting the Poor . . . and Yourself* (Chicago, IL: Moody, 2012), 64.

2. Cornel West, *Race Matters*, 25th Anniversary edition with new introduction (Boston: Beacon Press, 2017), 12.

3. Robertson McQuilkin and Paul Copan, *An Introduction to Biblical Ethics: Walking in the Way of Wisdom*, 3rd ed. (Downers Grove, IL: InterVarsity Press, 2014), 466.

CHAPTER 22: GUNS AND VIOLENCE

1. Rebecca M. Cunningham, Maureen A. Walton, and Patrick M. Carter, "The Major Causes of Death in Children and Adolescents in the United States," *New England Journal of Medicine* 379, no. 25 (December 20, 2018): 2468–2475, https://www.ncbi.nlm.nih.gov/pmc/articles /PMC6637963/.

2. Tim Walker, "Unannounced Active Shooter Drills Scaring Students without Making Them Safer," National Education Association, February 25, 2020, https://www.nea.org/advocating-for-change/new-from-nea/unannounced -active-shooter-drills-scaring-students-without.

3. Karen Swallow Prior, "Can Guns Be Pro-Life?," in *Cultural Engagement: A Crash Course in Contemporary Issues,* eds. Joshua D. Chatraw and Karen Swallow Prior (Grand Rapids, MI: Zondervan, 2019), 333.

4. J. Warner Wallace, "Is Jesus a Pacifist?," Cold-Case Christianity, October 6, 2020, https://coldcasechristianity.com/writings/is-jesus-a-pacifist/.

CHAPTER 23: IMMIGRATION

1. Jorge Ramos "We Are Going to Die in Here," *Texas Monthly,* May 2005, https://www.texasmonthly.com/politics/we-are-going-to-die-in-here/.

2. Howard Pankratz, "Gomez-Garcia Gets the Max: 80 Years," *Denver Post,* updated May 8, 2016, https://www.denverpost.com/2006/10/25 /gomez-garcia-gets-the-max-80-years/.

3. Martin Kasindorf, "Marine Lance Cpl. José Gutiérrez," Honor the Fallen, *Military Times,* accessed November 12, 2021, https://thefallen .militarytimes.com/marine-lance-cpl-jose-gutierrez/256506.

4. Markus Zehnder, *The Bible and Immigration: A Critical and Empirical Reassessment* (Eugene, OR: Pickwick Publications, 2021), 259.

5. Zehnder, *The Bible and Immigration,* 279.

6. M. Daniel Carroll R., *Christians at the Border: Immigration, the Church, and the Bible,* 2nd ed. (Grand Rapids, MI: Brazos, 2013), 122–123.

7. Scott B. Rae, *Moral Choices: An Introduction to Ethics,* 4th ed. (Grand Rapids, MI: Zondervan, 2018), 472.

CHAPTER 24: ARTIFICIAL INTELLIGENCE

1. There is good evidence to believe the soul is real. It makes sense of things like near-death experiences, our capacity to make choices, and the difference between mental and physical states. See the Dr. Sean McDowell YouTube channel: "What Is the Evidence for the Soul? A Conversation with J. P. Moreland," June 17, 2020, https://www.youtube.com/watch?v =oD7OCHl1odA.

2. Josefina Blattmann, "Netflix: Binging on the Algorithm," UX Planet, August 2, 2018, https://uxplanet.org/netflix-binging-on-the-algorithm -a3a74a6c1f59.

3. Jason Thacker, *The Age of AI: Artificial Intelligence and the Future of Humanity* (Grand Rapids, MI: Zondervan, 2020), 109.

4. Thacker, *The Age of AI,* 109.

5. Homeland Security, "Social Media Bots Overview," May 2018, https://niccs.us-cert.gov/sites/default/files/documents/pdf/ncsam_socialmediabots overview_508.pdf?trackDocs=ncsam_socialmediabotsoverview_508.pdf.

CHAPTER 26: A GUIDE FOR CONVERSATIONS

1. These questions were inspired by Tim Muehlhoff, "Christians in the Argument Culture: Apologetics as Conversation," in *A New Kind of Apologist*, ed. Sean McDowell (Eugene, OR: Harvest House, 2016), 21–28.

About the Author

⚡

DR. SEAN MCDOWELL is a gifted communicator with a passion for equipping the church, and young people in particular, to make the case for the Christian faith. He connects with audiences in a tangible way through humor and stories while imparting hard evidence and logical support for viewing all areas of life through a biblical worldview. Sean is an associate professor in the Christian Apologetics program at the Biola University Talbot School of Theology.

Sean still teaches one high school Bible class, which helps give him exceptional insight into the prevailing culture so he can impart his observations poignantly to fellow educators, pastors, and parents alike. In 2008, he received the Educator of the Year award for San Juan Capistrano, California. The Association of Christian Schools International awarded exemplary status to his apologetics training. Sean is listed among the top 100 apologists in the world. He graduated summa cum laude from Talbot Theological Seminary with a double master's degree in theology and philosophy. He earned a PhD in apologetics and worldview studies from Southern Baptist Theological Seminary in 2014.

Traveling throughout the United States and abroad, Sean speaks at camps, churches, schools, universities, and conferences. He has spoken for organizations including Focus on the Family, the Colson Center for Christian Worldview, Cru, Youth Specialties, Hume Lake Christian Camps, Fellowship of Christian Athletes, and the Association of Christian Schools International. Sean is the cohost of the *Think Biblically* podcast, which is one of the most popular podcasts on faith and cultural engagement.

Sean is the author, coauthor, or editor of more than twenty books, including *Chasing Love: Sex, Love, and Relationships in a Confused Culture, The Fate of the Apostles, So the Next Generation Will Know* (with J. Warner Wallace), *Evidence That Demands a Verdict* (with Josh McDowell), *Is God Just a Human Invention?* (with Jonathan Morrow), *Understanding Intelligent Design* (with William A. Dembski), and *Same-Sex Marriage: A Thoughtful Approach to God's Design for Marriage* (with John Stonestreet). Sean is the general editor for *A New Kind of Apologist, Apologetics for a New Generation, Sharing the Good News with Mormons*, and the *Apologetics Study Bible for Students*. Sean writes one of the leading apologetics blogs, which can be read at seanmcdowell.org.

Sean played college basketball at Biola University and was the captain his senior year on a team that went 30–7. In April 2000, Sean married his high school sweetheart, Stephanie. They have three children and live in San Juan Capistrano, California.

WANT TO FIND OUT MORE ABOUT SEAN AND HIS MINISTRY? VISIT SEANMCDOWELL.ORG.

Sean McDowell is a professor at Biola University and enjoys using social media to equip Christians with what they need to lovingly defend their faith.

Connect with Sean on YouTube, Instagram, TikTok, and Twitter @Sean_McDowell.

In addition to his role at Biola University, Sean speaks at churches and conferences nationwide. To contact Sean for a speaking engagement, or to see his schedule, check out SeanMcDowell.org.